Social Security
and Its Enemies

SOCIAL SECURITY

AND

ITS ENEMIES

The Case for America's Most Efficient Insurance Program

MAX J. SKIDMORE

Westview Press

A Member of the Perseus Books Group

Copyright © 1999 by Westview Press, A Member of the Perseus Books Group

Published in 1999 in the United States of America by Westview Press, 5500 Central Avenue, Boulder, Colorado 80301-2877, and in the United Kingdom by Westview Press, 12 Hid's Copse Road, Cumnor Hill, Oxford OX2 9JJ

Library of Congress Cataloging-in-Publication Data
Skidmore, Max J., 1933–
   Social security and its enemies : the case for America's most
efficient insurance program / Max J. Skidmore.
      p. cm.
   Includes bibliographical references and index.
   ISBN 0-8133-3663-5
   1. Social security—United States. I. Title.
HD7125.S565   1999
368.4'3'00973—dc21   99-17939
                                                                    CIP

The paper used in this publication meets the requirements of the American National Standard for Permanence of Paper for Printed Library Materials Z39.48-1984.

10   9   8   7   6   5   4   3   2   1

For Joey Skidmore
(one of rock and roll's most creative voices),
Faye, and their family—with assurance that
Social Security will be there for them

Contents

Preface
Social Security and Its Enemies

Everyone knows that Social Security is in danger—but almost no one really understands why. Contrary to popular belief, Social Security is not in danger from retiring baby boomers. In fact, in 2030 when the boomers have retired, the work force will contain a substantially *higher* percentage of the population than it did in the 1960s when the boomers were young. Nor does trouble arise from grasping greedy geezers or government theft of Social Security funds.

The real danger is not that Social Security is unsound, but that its enemies might convince the public to accept "reforms" that would destroy it. Who are the enemies? They are the ideologues and the selfish. The ideologues would eliminate government programs in the name of ideological purity. The selfish lust after the fortunes to be made if even a small portion of Social Security were "privatized." Neither group is concerned with the consequences of their actions for others.

The only true threat facing the system—apart from possible problems with Medicare—comes from a skillful and well financed propaganda campaign, a campaign that has convinced many citizens and policymakers that Social Security is in dire need of reform—that it must be "saved." A close look at most major "reforms" reveals that they are clever attacks designed to demolish the world's most successful and most efficient income-maintenance program. Chapter 8 deals with the special situation of Medicare.

America tends to be especially vulnerable to political rhetoric that uses the symbols of individualism. Such rhetoric can lead to public misunderstanding of government programs. The skillful use of rhetoric by Ronald Reagan and his political heirs has generated the perception of a Social Security crisis. That Social Security remains popular in the face of such an onslaught is a tribute to its soundness. That many people fail to recognize that a government program can be so efficient is the major danger.

There are many books about Social Security. Some are technical explanations of the system. Others are designed for scholarly specialists. *Social Security and Its Enemies* is different. It does explain the history and principles of the system, and it will certainly be useful in a variety of college and university classes. But its major importance is in countering the propaganda designed to destroy Social Security. It examines the sources of that propaganda, explains clearly why there is no crisis, and reveals the motives of the opponents.

Most books written for the public portray Social Security as fatally flawed. They suggest revisions that would reduce benefits, shrink Social Security into a welfare program limited to the very poor, or eliminate it entirely. These books result from the efforts of special interests that would benefit from dismantling a program that, in addition to being the most efficient and successful of its kind, is also the largest. These same special interests have poured forth a flood of articles calculated to convince the public that Social Security as we know it cannot survive.

Because of Social Security's popularity, much of the attack upon it masquerades as objective, nonpartisan, and impartial. This is shrewd strategy, and it often works. Sam Beard, for example, seeks to eliminate social insurance and replace it with private savings. Raising the false issue of "intergenerational equity" and addressing his appeals to the young, he likes to pretend that he is a liberal, and he has even succeeded in having one of his books listed in Amazon.com under the category: "Save Social Security Books."

Most notably successful, though, is a former secretary of commerce, Peter Peterson. Peterson—whose organization, the Concord Coalition, hides his ultraconservative agenda—is an anti-Social Security zealot. Presenting his Concord Coalition as an organization disinterestedly devoted to fiscal integrity and balanced budgets was a major triumph. Among other things, it led the Clinton administration to give the Concord Coalition joint authority along with the American Association of Retired Persons (AARP) to administer each regional forum that led up to the 1998 White House Conference on Social Security.

The success of the war against Social Security thus far can be gauged by the terms of the debate. On all sides, the question is, "How can Social Security be saved?" We almost never hear, "Is it really in trouble?" Even the AARP, in defending the system, accepts without question the projection that the current level of funding will be adequate only until 2032. Rarely is there an acknowledgment that the projection itself is highly questionable and that more optimistic—and more realistic—projections give indication of no trouble at all.

There have been a few voices of reason raised to counter the adverse propaganda, but very few. This book joins those few, but it also goes beyond them. In addition to explaining why Social Security is sound, it documents the covert war against social insurance that dates back to the passage of the Social Security Act in 1935. It explains how and why, after a long period of dormancy, the opposition emerged slowly from the underground in the 1960s and 1970s and burst forth from the shadows with a vengeance in the 1980s.

If this book succeeds in revealing to the public the true nature of the opposition to Social Security and in rekindling confidence in the strength and soundness of the program, it will have been worth writing.

If it succeeds in revealing to the public the true nature of the opposition and in halting further attacks on Social Security, whether by eliminating the opposition or by just driving it back underground, *Social Security and Its Enemies* will have achieved its purpose.

Max J. Skidmore

Acknowledgments

Many people have encouraged me in this study and have supplied me with information; I thank them all. I wish especially to thank my wife, Charlene, for so many things—including the wise suggestion that Westview Press would be an excellent choice as a publisher. She was right. I have worked with many editors, none better than Leo Wiegman. I especially thank him, as well as Kristin Milavec, project editor, and Silvine Marbury Farnell, the copy editor; they are outstanding.

Max J. Skidmore

Acknowledgments

Social Security
and Its Enemies

Myth Versus Reality in Social Security

It Ain't What People Don't Know

What if you up and die on me?" Tammy Whitebread was thirty-one, but Ron Taylor was fifty-five. Her question to Ron brought them to the altar. Most of their associates assumed Tammy and Ron, with two children, were already married. "Like many couples," said the *Kansas City Star's* feature on civil weddings, "they chose the courthouse in an attempt to keep the ceremony small, low-key, even a bit of a secret." After ten years as a family, the couple had as their "biggest reason for a quick courthouse connection: 'Social Security,'" Tammy said.[1]

She wanted assurance that she and the children would be fully eligible for benefits if Ron were to die. Fortunately, she was aware of Social Security's value. She might not have made so sound a judgment if she had relied on television, magazine, and newspaper coverage for her information—including the lurid and alarming reports about Social Security that surface regularly in the *Star* itself.

What Can Americans Really Expect from Social Security?

What is it that Americans can expect from Social Security? The realities are sharply—and fortunately—different from what the headlines suggest.

Many people, especially the young, fear that it "won't be there" when they need it. This fear is the natural result of a coherent and well-financed campaign by Social Security's enemies to kill the system. To understand what is happening, it is necessary to examine the criticisms thoroughly, to study the nature of Social Security, and to brush aside propaganda and look at the real situation.

The late humorist Will Rogers is supposed to have remarked, "it ain't what people don't know that's so dangerous—it's what people know that just ain't so." That certainly is true about Social Security. Looking at the real situation, as this brief book makes clear, reveals some unexpected things. Among them:

- Despite the projections and the virtually universal assumptions of journalists and television commentators, it is highly unlikely that the trust funds where the money that runs the system accumulates will be depleted in 2029, 2032, or anytime. For that depletion to happen, the American economy would have to perform much more poorly than it normally does, and it would have to keep up that poor performance over an unusually long period.
- Despite allegations from opponents, the trust funds do contain real value, not "worthless IOUs." The government bonds that the trust funds hold have value as secure as the dollar bills that every citizen holds—and they are secure for the same reasons.
- Despite criticism of governmental borrowing from the trust funds, those funds could not just sit uninvested. Simply to invest them in the private market not only would introduce risk that government bonds do not carry, but also—because of their huge amounts—could give government control of private markets. President Clinton did suggest in his 1999 State of the Union address that a portion of the funds be privately invested.

If the portion remains small, the risk would be acceptable, he believes, in order to obtain the probability of greater return from the stock market. He argues that an independent body could administer the investments without the danger of government control. Nevertheless, the potential dangers outweigh any possible benefits, and in any case such investment is unnecessary.

Many people misunderstand the true nature of the trust funds' use of government bonds. The bonds in the trust funds do mature and do pay interest back into the funds. It is important to recognize that the trust funds did not create government borrowing. If they had not been available, the government still would have had to borrow, but the borrowing would have been from private investors. At the time when government borrowing was skyrocketing—in the 1980s—much of it would have been from Arab oil sheiks and Japanese industrialists. It all still would have to be paid back, but in that case, the funds would have been flowing abroad instead of into the Social Security system.

- Despite the frightening use of demographic statistics, the number of workers supporting each beneficiary will decline only slightly over the next three decades, and at its low point will still be greater than it was in the 1960s. Why? Because of the huge influx of women into the workforce.

- Despite the attempt to convince citizens that Social Security offers poor value, any objective study demonstrates that it offers exceptionally good value and will continue to do so.

- Despite the arguments of the critics, it is not wrong or unfair to pay benefits to those who are wealthy, who do not "need" them, any more than it is wrong or unfair for a company pension plan to do so. Building in "need" as a criterion for benefits would require the majority to contribute for a lifetime to a program that would not benefit them. It would also require a person seeking benefits to go through the humiliating process of checking with a welfare office and proving poverty. Social Security's universal coverage is its greatest strength.

- Despite the rosy promises of its advocates, "privatization" does not guarantee a better return, a good return, or even any return. It does guarantee widely varied results, including the possibility of loss of investment. Most proposals also guarantee the loss or drastic reduction of Social Security's life insurance and disability insurance protections. Duplicating these protections would require private policies exceeding a half million dollars. Additionally, most proposals would mean the loss of Medicare protection.

- Despite the glowing propaganda about the success of privatization in other countries, the results of foreign attempts to privatize range from doubtful to catastrophic. For example, the propagandists loudly praised Great Britain's partially privatized system as a model until the *Wall Street Journal* embarrassed them with its page-one report on 10 August 1998 under the headline, "Social Security Switch in U.K. Is Disastrous; A Caution to the U.S.?" Sub-headlines read, "Many Britons Suffer Losses on 'Personal Pensions'; Insurers Have to Pay Up" and "Tab May Reach $18 Billion." Did the "privatizers" admit their error? No. Their response was to become strangely silent about the British system, but to continue their campaign—as witnessed by Tom Miller's article, "How to Get Real Social Security," in the mass-circulation *Reader's Digest* for December 1998.

- Despite the apparent plausibility of the calculations the privatizers make to show that workers will be better off under a privatized system, those calculations are in fact based on false assumptions. They assume, for example, that without Social Security, each worker would have not only the 6.2 percent Social Security taxes to "invest," but the employer's 6.2 percent match as well. (Some have even argued for the full 7.65 percent plus the match, which includes the Medicare tax.) Why? Because "the match is a part of the salary." Anyone who believes that employers would voluntarily add that amount to the employees' take-home pay if Social Security were eliminated forgets the current climate of downsizing, in which employers compete to slash jobs and often to convert as many as possible of those remaining to part-time and temporary positions that do not carry expensive fringe benefits. So the critics' calculations involve doubling the amount of money that actually would be available to invest. They also tend to use as an example a single worker whose average lifetime wage is at or above the maximum for Social Security taxation. Using as an example a worker at the top of the income groups always will produce a less favorable result than using one at the middle or lower, because lower paid workers receive a greater return in relation to their payments than more highly paid workers do. They do so as the result of a policy explicitly designed to reduce poverty. Moreover, most workers are not single and therefore have protection for survivors and can expect a spouse's benefit. Even the single worker has coverage against disability. Privatizers do not figure this coverage, with a value greater than a $200,000 policy, into the calculations. Equally misleading is the privatizers' tendency to ignore the inflation protection built into Social Security benefits. Those benefits are indexed to inflation; returns from fixed investments are not.

- Despite the allegations of the critics, Social Security does not involve "intergenerational inequities"—a notion that is not only suspect but vague and probably impossible to define. Nor does Social Security involve the unjust enrichment of one economic class at the expense of another. Virtually the entire population is covered, deferring consumption in order to receive not only retirement benefits, but also health benefits, coverage against disability, and protection for survivors. Younger workers are not only protecting themselves and their dependents by their Social Security payments, they are also ensuring in most cases that they do not have to care directly for elderly parents and grandparents, as pre-Social Security generations were required to do.

This list could go on, but these points should be enough to cause some rethinking about the dire predictions relating to Social Security. Many of them are worth repeating, and so they will be repeated in the following discussion.

Why Is Social Security Still So Popular?

Remarkably, in spite of the campaign and the skepticism, studies consistently rate Social Security as highly popular. In fact it is arguably the most popular program that the United States government has ever enacted. There are good reasons for its popularity. Before Social Security, poverty was a common condition of the elderly. Now, the aged are financially much better off. In lifting the elderly as a group from destitution to relative comfort, Social Security has done—and is doing—precisely what the country designed it to do: It is enhancing security by providing benefits.

Does this mean that Social Security is enriching the elderly beyond the rest of the population? Are Americans at the mercy of a bunch of "Greedy Geezers," as the *New Republic* called them a few years back, a charge many others have echoed? Not at all. There is still a greater rate of poverty among the elderly than among other *adult* Americans.[2]

It bears repeating that Social Security's benefits are not limited to the elderly. They do provide a floor for retirement income, but they also protect Americans against loss of income resulting from disability, and they protect children and caregivers of those children in the event of a breadwinner's death. According to the Social Security Administration's Office of the Actuary, it would require a policy of $207,000 to duplicate the disability coverage, and one of $307,000 to equal the protection for survivors.[3] Social Security also protects the younger generation indirectly by making it likely that its parents and grandparents will be self-sufficient. The system ultimately helps nearly everyone, and its benefits come without the need to demonstrate poverty.

Americans have earned their benefits. They are not charity. That is the major reason why the system remains so popular. Could it remain popular if the American public reacted in outrage (as its enemies hope they will) to the fact "that millionaires receive Social Security"? Since they, too, have paid in, is there any good reason why millionaires should not receive benefits? Wealthy retirees receive private pensions, even when the companies from which they retired complain of low profits, as noted above, and no one argues that private pensions should be means tested.

If Americans ever give in to the plea that the wealthy should not receive benefits, would the strong incentives *not* to save (because doing so might make it impossible to collect Social Security later on) damage an economy that already suffers from a rate of saving that nearly all economists believe is too low? If it were necessary for everyone to go through the humiliating process of proving poverty in order to receive benefits, could middle-class support for Social Security continue, or would it vanish overnight? If that support vanished, there is no doubt that the system would vanish also.

Does this mean that the critics from both extremes of the political spectrum are correct when they call Social Security a "middle-class program?" It does not. Surely the program helps the middle classes, but it helps the wealthy as well—and it helps the poor most of all. It is far from perfect. The taxes hit the poor harder than the middle class, and hit the middle class harder than the wealthy, but the poor receive considerably more in benefits, in relation to the taxes they pay, than other income groups do. In addition, the earned income tax credit offsets FICA taxes for the working poor.

The public once understood the nature of the Social Security system. Now attacks and misleading rhetoric from opponents—and from some misguided supporters, as well—have obscured this understanding. Social Security is a program not merely for the middle class, but for the whole of American society. The public needs once again to understand this fact.

Many figures in prominent political positions today would be delighted to see the entire system including Medicare vanish. Of course generally they cannot say so because they fear public reaction. They content themselves, therefore, with calling for means tests and benefit cuts. They argue that they intend only to "save the system."

Consider the controversy in 1995 and 1996 over whether the Medicare proposals that President Clinton vetoed would have provided "cuts" in the program as the president said, or merely "reductions in the rate of growth," as supporters of the reductions alleged when they argued that they were attempting to "save the system." The Republicans were correct when they pointed out that their proposals would have resulted in increasing the money being spent on Medicare. Thus they could claim that they proposed merely reductions in the rate of growth, certainly not cuts.

What they attempted to hide, however, was that inflation and growing population require growth to maintain the same level of benefits. Their proposals would have resulted in benefit reductions. Undoubtedly the program would have continued to grow in the sense that the total dollars spent would have been greater, but it would have provided considerably less to each person. Providing less—reducing benefits—is a rather good definition of a "cut," and all parties to the debate were well aware that the proposals would have reduced benefits. It is in this sense that "cut" was an appropriate description of the proposals.

The system covers a huge number of Americans. Now, virtually all can look forward to receiving benefits. Remarkably, those benefits are provided at an administrative cost of less than one cent of every tax dollar collected.[4] That is far more efficient than any private insurance program—so much so that no private insurance program is even in the same league, let alone ballpark.

The very best private insurance companies take many times what Social Security does out of every dollar paid in. Even a well-managed profitmaking HMO returns less than ninety cents of each dollar received in benefits. It's a novel idea for Americans—government being more efficient than private industry. In the case of Social Security, though, that clearly is the case. This observation is true not only in the United States, but generally around the world.

The hidden—and, to Americans, unbelievable—truth is that government in general operates to provide benefits much more efficiently than any private plan can. This includes health benefits. Government provides health care, when it does so, at much less cost than private industry does. The private health care system in the United States costs more for what it delivers than any health care system in the world. The Medicare system delivers vastly more for every dollar paid in than the best managed health plan can accomplish. Even the much maligned Medicaid program (which provides care for the poor) does so.

Yet we hear that government can never do anything right. When we hear this, we are inclined to think, "Yeah, that's right!" We rarely think in detail. We ignore such things as, for example, constructing the Panama Canal, winning two world wars and a cold war, putting a man on the moon, setting up the Internet—and we even ignore the fact that the Social Security system has never failed to provide its benefit checks when due. That is something that the insurance industry certainly cannot say of itself. It would come as a shock, perhaps, to many Americans to discover that most retired people do not receive private retirement benefits at all. Something like 92 percent of American retirees receive Social Security, while only about 31 percent receive anything from private pensions.[5]

In response to propaganda favoring privatization, we hear people say, "Social Security's a great idea, but it's going broke, and won't be there long." As I have said, Social Security remains popular, but it is obviously true that confidence in the stability and future of the system has declined. Is our declining confidence the result of any major troubles in the system that we have overlooked until now, or does it result entirely, or almost entirely, from exaggerating the troubles that the system faces?

What Happened to the Surplus?
Or, the Case of the Curious Calculations

In the early 1980s, Social Security faced troubles with cash flow in its OASI Trust Fund. Gleeful politicians may have been happy to exaggerate, but the troubles were real and led to the creation of a 1982–1983 National Commission on Social Security Reform, chaired by Alan Greenspan. The Greenspan Commission's recommendations became the basis for the restructuring of the system in 1983.

Among other things, the revisions led to a gradual increase in the full retirement age from sixty-five to sixty-seven, and mandated a schedule of tax increases that culminated in today's 7.65 percent tax on employees with its employer match. These changes were calculated to bring the system not only into balance, but into surplus. That projection was for an actuarial surplus of .02 percent over the seventy-five-year period—that is, indefinitely. Recent projections, however, have projected not a surplus, but a deficit that in the 1998 report was 2.19 percent. Were the 1983 projections too optimistic? Have economic conditions not lived up to the 1983 expectations? On the contrary, economic conditions have been *more favorable* than projected in 1983. The performance of the trust funds likewise has been *more favorable* than the 1983 projections had anticipated. Where did the surplus go?

Answering this question requires a look at the actual projections—and a look at those projections makes the answer quite clear. Nothing has happened demographically or in the economy to make the projected surplus vanish. The only thing that has changed is the method used to arrive at the projections. In fact, all the indications have become progressively more favorable—except for the calculations themselves!

In the 1991 report, for example, the trustees admitted that "the new test, while more complicated than prior tests, is also more stringent."[6] Not only were the tests more stringent, the trustees reduced the number of optional scenarios that they reported. Whether they intended to or not, this gave the impression of greater precision. "It may be noted," said the report, "that recent annual reports, through the 1990 report, included four alternative sets of assumptions, including two intermediate alternatives, II-A and II-B. Beginning with this report, a single intermediate set, alternative II, is shown."[7] Among the economic assumptions required to arrive at the projections are "gross national product, labor force, unemployment, average earnings, productivity, inflation, fertility, mortality, net immigration, marriage, divorce, retirement patterns, and disability incidence and termination."[8]

The reporters and policymakers who assume without question that "the trust funds are to be exhausted in 2032" should ask themselves just how accurately these factors can be predicted ten or twenty years into the future, let alone seventy-five. Consider, for example, that about a year before the government announced a balanced budget, our best economic projections anticipated budget deficits years into the future; consider that no one predicted, or has yet adequately explained, the sharp and steady drop in crime in America in recent years; consider also that the most sophisticated analysis was unable to predict even the dissolution of the Soviet Union, one of the two superpowers on earth. Then ask whether projections in 1924 could have anticipated conditions in 1999 (a seventy-five-year projection), or even whether you would wish to rely on 1966 projections to draw conclusions about 1999 (a thirty-three-year projection). If projections of this kind raise doubts, so, too, should projections of trust-fund exhaustion in 2032 (another thirty-three-year projection)—especially when the calculations have been based on increasingly stringent tests.

Among those increasingly stringent tests is a requirement that the balance in the trust funds at the end of the projection period be adequate to cover the full costs of a year's benefits. Imagine the difficulties if personal finances were calculated in this manner. To avoid bankruptcy, a household would have to have enough money on 31 December to pay all living expenses for the next year without any income. Yet this is the test of solvency applied to Social Security, a test that considers a deficit to exist if there is not "a trust fund level at the end of the period equal to about 100 percent of the following year's expenditures."[9] In the trustees' words, "a targeted ending trust fund level of 1 year's expenditures is considered to be an adequate reserve for unforeseen contingencies; thus, in addition to the total outgo during the projection period, the summarized cost rate includes the cost of reaching and maintaining a target trust fund ratio of 100 percent through the end of the projection period."[10]

The trustees recognize the tentative nature of their projections, even if journalists and propagandists do not. "The resulting estimates should be interpreted with care," they warned in 1991. "In particular, they are not intended to be exact predictions of the future status of the OASDI program."[11] Yet that is precisely the way in which Social Security's opponents use them.

Consider, for example, the comments about Social Security by Susan Dentzer, a cautious writer who was formerly economics columnist for *U.S. News and World Report* and is currently a correspondent for *The News Hour with Jim Lehrer*. In a 1998 discussion published by the national Academy of Social Insurance, she warned against "cover stories that crow about how Social Security is irretrievably broken," as well as against what she called the other extreme, which sees all "privatization or partial privatization proposals as simply the result of the stealthy machinations of Wall Street." She asserted that the "press should acknowledge the uncertainties and resist unequivocal doom-and-gloom scenarios about the future of Social Security. This will be tough going," she said, "since to date the doom-and-gloom school appears to have thoroughly captured and dominated much of the press and public opinion. A case in point is the many books and treatises written by investment banker Peter Peterson, which have been excerpted time and again in many publications."[12]

She cautioned that "projections about the potential future underfunding of Social Security are not necessarily wrong," but admitted that "we cannot say with 100 percent certainty that they are right, either. We do not know whether any of the most dire fiscal outcomes that we think might come to pass will in fact come to pass. We cannot say what the future will look like." In fact, she went on to say, "Few policymakers will admit this publicly, so it is up to journalists to help fill this void. After all, as the National Academy of Social Insurance's own Robert Myers, formerly deputy commissioner of Social Security (and long-time chief actuary of the Social Security Administration), has pointed out in congressional testimony, under the low-cost estimate of Social Security prepared by the system's actuaries, the program is projected to experience no long-term financing problem whatsoever. Yet when was the last time you read in the popular press that under some plausible—if not especially likely—circumstances, Social Security might never be in trouble at all? I confess," she said, "that not even I have raised this possibility in any of my written work to date on Social Security."[13]

Dentzer deserves credit for her recognition that the press has been irresponsible in dealing with Social Security, for her admission that she also has failed to report the full picture, and for her skewering of scaremongers such as Peter Peterson. Her conviction that the more optimistic projections are "not especially likely," though, apparently continues to make it difficult for her to present the full situation to popular audiences. The journal of the American Association of Retired Persons (AARP), *Modern Maturity*, presented an article of hers as a special report on Social Security in its January–February, 1999, issue. She carefully dealt with questions regarding privatization, but again continued to refer to "the system's projected long-term deficit," discussing it in detail as though it were definite. Nowhere did she even suggest that there may be no long-term trouble at all. So, one year after she implicitly apologized for not having presented the full picture in her popular writing, she continues to treat the intermediate projection as though it were precise, and hardly open to question.

Dentzer might refresh her memory by referring to the trustees' 1998 report, which included an even more detailed warning than the one cited above. It spoke of "the uncertainty inherent in projections of this type and length. In general, a greater degree of confidence can be placed in the assumptions and estimates for the earlier years than for the later years," the report said. "Nonetheless," it admitted, "even for the earlier years, the estimates are only an indication of the expected trend and potential range of future program experience."[14]

Those who would dismantle, or radically revise, a superbly functioning program based on such a shaky rationale should look even further into the reports. As the 1998 version made plain, the intermediate projection which called for trust fund exhaustion in 2032 assumed a rate of gross domestic product (GDP) growth far below actual experience. From 1999 on through 2075, the *highest* anticipated growth rate was 2.0 percent, and that was to occur only in five of the years.

Yet their own figures show that the actual experience has been vastly better. In only five years since 1960 has the rate been 2.0 percent or below; thirty-four of the thirty-nine years have been above their projected maximum, usually far above. In other words, the projections assume that the *best* years in the future will be far worse than the *average* years in the past. The projected figures for inflation, similarly, are far more pessimistic than actual experience.[15]

Moreover, in summarizing each of the reports from 1988 through 1998, the trustees candidly described nearly all of the various changes in each of the projections as resulting, not from the actual experience of the trust funds, not from the real world, but from "assumptions and methods," "changes in economic assumptions," and the like.[16] One of those assumptions is an ever-increasing life span. It is dubious—if not biologically impossible—that life expectancy will steadily increase forever, but such a notion undergirds the calculations. This assumption means that each year's projection will contain a more expensive year at the end of the valuation period than the projection for the previous year. In other words, the projections assume that the simple passage of time will cause costs to increase steadily.

The trustees issue annual projections because the law requires them to do so. Until the opponents of Social Security began to use them in their campaign to undermine the system, the projections rarely attracted attention. Now, thanks to the propaganda by the opponents, even most of Social Security's supporters accept the intermediate projections, however questionable, as prophecy rather than as qualified possibilities. The feeble defense of these supporters tends not to question the projections, but rather to protest that the system, after 2032, will still be able to pay three-fourths of its benefits. This is a tribute to the success of the critics, who themselves could hardly damn the system more strongly with praises so faint.

Those few analysts who have recognized how unrealistic the trustees' projections actually are and how those projections play into the hands of Social Security's greatest enemies, sometimes wonder at the motivation behind them. We do not know what those motivations have been, nor is it likely that we ever could know. Even though some of the more conspiratorially-minded analysts sense an intent to harm the system or to encourage an accumulation of funds greater than necessary for the program in order to mask government spending, it is better not to fall into that trap, but simply to assume the best: to assume that the motivation has been to be professional and to err on the side of caution.

It takes little research to demonstrate that the last few years have seen concerted and consistent attacks upon Social Security by political forces that have always opposed government activity in support of the Constitution's charge to "promote the general welfare," forces that have become emboldened in the last couple of decades. The existence of a campaign against Social Security is clear, and it is a serious political effort.

The existence of such a campaign does not, of course, prove that no flaws exist in the Social Security system, but the truth is that the flaws are minor. In fact, they are so minor that any major attempt to "reform" or to "save" the system is almost guaranteed to have destructive results. Social Security is a huge program, but it is small in comparison with the total American economy. Even if the projections of increasing benefits turn out to be correct—and there are good reasons to believe that they are much too pessimistic—the increase between now and 2070 would turn out to be only from 4.8 percent of the gross domestic product (GDP) to 6.8 percent.

This 2 percent of GDP increase is "less than the variations in the share of the GDP devoted to defense since the mid-1970s."[17] The economy is capable of handling such fluctuations quite well—and in fact has done so.

Nevertheless, because of the tremendous flood of negative propaganda, restoring full public confidence in the system probably will require more than mere reassurances. Social Security's enemies have skillfully created fears for the future. Reasonable as it may be to point out that projections are unreliable, or to remind the public that a better indication of future performance is the excellent performance of the past, some action may be necessary to convince the public that all is well.

There are in fact some incremental changes that could provide absolute assurance for the trust funds without changing the nature of Social Security or damaging the system. These changes include lifting the cap on earnings subject to taxation, raising the interest rate on the bonds in the trust funds, earmarking certain portions of the income tax to the trust funds, and—as President Clinton recommended in his 1998 State of the Union address—earmarking a portion of the budget surplus for the trust funds. Chapter 5 discusses these beneficial changes in more detail

In the meantime it is necessary to examine Social Security, to look at the system carefully. Evaluating the fears and criticisms requires an understanding of the nature of social insurance. First we will examine what the system is, how it operates, and how it came to be what it is. Only then are we truly in a position to analyze in depth what the critics are saying, and to understand why they are saying it.

How Social Security Works and What It Provides

Workers become eligible for benefits by accumulating "credits" (that is, by earning wages of a certain amount in covered employment). Because of inflation, the amount of earnings required to establish a credit increases each year. For 1999, the minimum amount required is $740; a worker may accumulate a credit for each $740 up to four credits for a year. Eligibility generally is based on forty credits, or ten years of earnings, although there are exceptions in certain instances. For example, the survivors of a very young worker who dies may be eligible for benefits even though the worker had been in the work force for a much shorter time than ten years.

For 1999, the tax rates are 7.65 percent on the first $72,600 of income; the employer pays another 7.65 percent to match the worker's payment. Workers and employers each pay 1.45 percent above the $72,600 limit for Medicare. Those who are self-employed pay 15.3 percent on the first $72,600 of earnings, and 2.9 percent above that amount. Each dollar of tax on the first $72,600 is allocated to one of three trust funds: seventy cents for old-age and survivors insurance, nineteen cents for hospital insurance (Medicare), and eleven cents for disability insurance. The trust funds pay benefits and administrative costs, and they invest their huge surpluses in the safest investments possible, U.S. government bonds, which regularly pay interest back into the trust funds. Despite fears that the "government has spent all the money," the trust funds are intact. They have no more been "raided" than have the funds of a citizen who invests money in savings bonds.

The benefits available from the Social Security system thus include much more than the familiar retirement benefits for workers and their dependents, but those benefits are still the heart of the program. They are available to workers who retire at age sixty-five, or at a reduced level to those who retire as young as sixty-two. Workers who do not retire until after sixty-five will have their benefit levels increased for every year they delay retirement until they are seventy. Spouses of retired workers can receive full benefits at the age of sixty-five (usually one-half of the benefits paid to the retired worker), or can apply for a reduced benefit at age sixty-two. Note that for those born in 1938 or later, the age for full retirement begins gradually to rise, becoming sixty-seven for those born in, or after, 1960.

A person has the option of retiring on his or her own wage record or on that of the spouse, whichever is greater, but cannot receive benefits on both records. However, a spouse can retire at age sixty-two with a reduced benefit on his or her own record, and then at age sixty-five switch to a full benefit based on the wage record of the spouse, if that benefit would be greater. A divorced spouse who is not currently married can receive benefits on a worker's record, just as if he or she were still married, provided that the marriage lasted ten years or more (or regardless of the length of marriage if the divorced spouse is still caring for the worker's child and that child receives benefits). The requirements otherwise are the same as for current spouses. An important thing to note is that this provision is no threat to the current spouse: payments to a divorced spouse have no effect upon those to a current spouse and do not count against the family maximum.

Also important are Social Security's life insurance elements, which discussions frequently overlook. They are substantial. In 1993, Social Security provided Americans with some $12.1 trillion in life insurance protection. That exceeded by "$1.3 trillion the combined value of all private life insurance policies of all types in force in the United States."[18] Spouses of deceased workers may receive survivors benefits when they reach sixty-five, or reduced benefits as young as age sixty. If they are disabled, they can also receive benefits beginning at the age of fifty. Children of deceased workers receive Social Security benefits if they are unmarried and under eighteen, or until nineteen if they are still in school. (Previously they could receive benefits until age twenty-one if they were in college, but Congress at the request of the Reagan administration eliminated the college benefits in 1981.) Surviving children who were disabled before reaching the age of twenty-two can receive disability benefits at any age. The spouse of a deceased worker receives benefits as a mother or father if providing care for the worker's children who have not yet reached the age of sixteen. If a deceased worker had dependent parents sixty-two or older, they can receive benefits.

Disability benefits at one time required "permanent and total disability." Now, however, a worker whose impairment may prevent engaging in any "substantial" work for at least a year may be eligible. The definition of "substantial" would mean as a rule that the person is incapable of earning $500 or more a month. Additionally, benefits may be available if the ailment is one from which death may be anticipated. The requirements are quite strict, both medically and in terms of eligibility for coverage. To be covered, a worker who is under the age of twenty-four must have six credits in the three years immediately prior to the onset of the disability. Workers aged twenty-four to thirty-one must have credits for half the time (that is, an average of at least two credits per year) between the attainment of age twenty-one and the onset of the disability. Those thirty-one or older must have a total of credits that increases gradually with age (from twenty at age forty-two, for example, to forty at age sixty-two or above), but there is another strict requirement. The worker must have earned twenty credits in the ten years immediately preceding the onset of the disability.

The health benefits program, Medicare, comes in two segments. Part A is hospital insurance. This coverage provides benefits paid for from the Medicare portion of Social Security taxes. Part B is medical insurance, which provides payments for bills from physicians. The beneficiary pays a monthly premium for Part B coverage, and thus has the option of rejecting it. A covered worker may enroll for Medicare at the age of sixty-five, even if he or she delays applying for other Social Security benefits.

Medicare benefits are extensive, but they are limited. Hospital benefits include payment for all covered services for the first sixty days of a stay, except for a deductible. For days sixty-one through ninety, benefits are the same except that the patient must pay a daily co-insurance amount. Hospital benefits end after the ninetieth day and do not resume until the beginning of another "benefit period," which starts after sixty days of no hospitalization. There is an exception to the end of benefits at ninety days. Each beneficiary has a lifetime total of sixty "reserve days," which can be used to extend a ninety-day stay in the hospital.

Under certain circumstances, Medicare will pay for skilled nursing care for up to one hundred days in an approved facility following a hospital stay. The first twenty days of such care are covered in full; the remaining eighty days require payment of a daily co-insurance amount. There is no coverage for custodial care, but under certain conditions Medicare does cover the full cost for home health visits from an approved home health agency. Numerous other items fall outside Medicare's coverage. Nursing homes are excluded, except after a hospital stay. There is no coverage for routine dental care, for dentures, eyeglasses, or hearing aids, no coverage for most prescription drugs, or for most immunizations, or for most routine examinations. Medicare will also pay for hospice care for terminally ill Medicare patients, under certain circumstances. The patient's physician and the hospice medical director both must certify that the patient has a life expectancy of six months or less, the patient must agree in writing to accept hospice care instead of standard Medicare benefits, and the care must be in a Medicare approved hospice.

Part B of Medicare, medical insurance, covers bills from physicians and many other items not included under hospital insurance. In general, in any year the patient must first pay a certain amount, the deductible, before benefits begin. Then, Medicare pays 80 percent of the covered charges for the remainder of the year.

The Social Security Administration has numerous pamphlets available free of charge that provide clear explanation of the various benefits, eligibility requirements, and the like.

Social Security replaces 43 percent of preretirement income for the average retired American and an average of 58 percent for low income retirees. It succeeds in "keeping tens of millions of Americans out of poverty."[19] It is responsible for a dramatic drop in the poverty rate among the elderly, but Social Security alone is certainly not sufficient to provide a comfortable living—or even the necessities.[20] Its benefits are modest, but vital.

Despite the importance of Social Security, its practicality, and its unparalleled efficiency, it was not easy to establish it in America. An understanding of the forces against it and what was required to overcome them will help in understanding why Social Security is under attack now, so in the next chapter I shall examine both the history and the opposition in some detail.

2
The Gospel of Wealth Amid Acres of Diamonds

More than many other societies, America has found it difficult to deal with questions of providing economic well-being for all of its citizens. As early as 1798, Thomas Paine set forth many of his radical economic ideas in *Agrarian Justice*—ideas that if implemented would have provided a social security system. Yet more than a century later, such American pioneers of social insurance as I. M. Rubinow, Paul Douglas, and Abraham Epstein continued to sound extreme to their fellow citizens.

By the first three decades of the twentieth century, there was ample European precedent for social insurance. Germany, in fact, had put extensive social insurance systems in place in 1883, under Bismarck. In the Western Hemisphere, Uruguay was an early pioneer. Foreign examples did not, however, seem to impress Americans. The belief was widespread that individual initiative was all that was required for virtually anyone to succeed in the American scheme of things. At the same time, pride in all things American did not keep Americans from holding their state and its functionaries in low esteem.[1] Such attitudes are if anything even worse now than previously and help to explain why the United States has adopted fewer, and less extensive, social programs than other advanced industrial countries.

Conditions Leading to Social Security

In the early years of industrialism, with its unsettled conditions that forced many rural people into crowded cities, there were no programs such as Social Security to help relieve economic distress. Vast new fortunes emerged, but so did unprecedented numbers of the very poor. The extremes of wealth and poverty that emerged as states industrialized brought protest movements in the late nineteenth century. These took many forms, both here and abroad. States dealt harshly with anarchist protest—as one might expect given anarchism's hostility to the idea of the state itself. Socialist movements became strong in some countries, but in America socialist successes were minimal. Even Christian socialism, which preached cooperation and love as opposed to what it viewed as the selfishness of competition, made little headway except briefly, and in a few church groups.

There were few calls for true social programs. Justification for unlimited accumulation of wealth as the prime social value was considerably more widespread than criticism, receiving support from the Social Darwinists that purported to be scientific. Others attempted to provide an ethical basis. The first such efforts were based in religion. Mark Hopkins, president of Williams College, argued that accumulation of property was necessary in order to benefit others. Much more crude were Russell H. Conwell's "Acres of Diamonds" speeches. Conwell, the founder and first president of Temple University, gave the speech to countless numbers of eager listeners.

Religion, he said, did not merely permit that one become rich, it demanded it! Accumulation of wealth was a duty, not a privilege. The poorest person in America could become rich and do so honestly and quickly. There was no excuse for poverty, which resulted only from one's own shortcomings or those of someone else. It was a sin to be poor, or even to sympathize with those who were poor, because poverty was invariably a punishment from God. The basis for the speech was the tale of a man who sold his land to seek riches. He wandered throughout a disappointing life, only to learn finally that the world's richest diamond mine had been discovered—on the land that he had squandered. Riches, Conwell preached, are in one's own backyard.

Such ideas are cruelly unrealistic, especially in a complex modern world, but they were highly popular as the twentieth century approached. It is tempting to write them off as reflecting the conditions of an unsettled time that had not developed an adequate understanding of the social and economic forces that were bringing radical change. Unfortunately, these and similar ideas have never been completely dismissed, and they have reemerged with force in recent years, as a cursory review of political speeches and leadership training courses will demonstrate.

The "robber barons"—as those American capitalists of the late nineteenth century who became wealthy by deliberate exploitation are called—felt no sense of social responsibility, but this lack of understanding of what they owed society did not include all industrialists, or "captains of industry," some of whom did have a sense of obligation. Prominent among them was the steel tycoon, Andrew Carnegie. After becoming one of the wealthiest persons in American history, Carnegie became the most articulate spokesman for the "gospel of wealth." In 1900 he wrote a book by that title, in which he called upon those of wealth to contribute to society and live without ostentation. He ably defended the system even while conceding that it was not perfect, and he lived up to his principles by constructing public libraries, endowing philanthropic foundations, establishing educational institutions, and otherwise using his wealth to benefit society. Others, such as John D. Rockefeller, who created the Rockefeller Foundation and endowed the University of Chicago, followed his lead. A contemporary example is the media mogul Ted Turner, who has made enormous philanthropic grants. In August 1996 he called upon others with huge wealth to do the same and charged that they tended to horde their wealth because of preoccupation with—and he was serious—retaining their status on the list of the richest people in the world.

Steps Toward Social Security in America

It was the Great Depression of the 1930s that shook the confidence of many Americans in the ability of their country to provide conditions of abundance without governmental action. It became increasingly evident to them that economic individualism and political liberties were not sufficient by themselves to ensure economic well-being in a complex society, but it required a disastrous collapse of the country's economic structure to bring about such a recognition. The conditions were so extreme that one of every four—or even every three—workers was unable to find any work at all. Even then, the abstract idea of government activity continued to raise questions.

Today the purely ideological (and essentially meaningless) question of how large government should be often receives more attention when considering a policy initiative than the effect of the policy itself. From a practical point of view the important question regarding a policy should be, "Will it make things better or worse?" not whether it affects the size of government. In the 1930s the emergency was so clearly evident that Americans accepted the New Deal, oriented to action rather than ideology, which emerged to counter the crisis. The New Deal brought forth the Social Security Act of 1935, which set up the system that may well lay claim to being the most popular government program in American history.

The term "social security" can be defined in various ways, and can include many things. Broadly interpreted, it encompasses all social welfare measures. In a stricter sense, it refers to the programs authorized by the Social Security Act. For most Americans, though, it has an even stricter meaning: the contributory social insurance programs—old age, disability, and survivors' insurance; it can also include the health benefits coverage of the Medicare program.

Despite American discomfort with government action, the Social Security Act did not emerge from a vacuum. The idea of involving the government in ensuring basic economic security for its citizens was not completely new in American history. In 1909, a White House Conference on Care of Dependent Children gave some impetus to the idea of governmental pensions or allowances to widows with dependent children. The first of the mothers' pension plans was established in Denver under the leadership of Gertrude Vaile, who had been active in the Charity Organization Society movement and had studied under one of its most prominent figures, Mary Richmond.

In 1914, writing in Paul Kellogg's magazine of social reform, *The Survey*, Vaile outlined the difficulties facing those who hoped for similar programs. She wrote that apathy was prevalent and only meager results were likely. A number of states did pass laws, but many of them did no more than authorize localities to establish programs if they chose.

There was ferment in the years following the 1909 White House Conference. Numerous progressive associations and groups were bringing together social workers, such as Jane Addams and Grace and Edith Abbott, with such other influential figures as Eleanor Roosevelt, Newton D. Baker, Louis Brandeis, and the prominent University of Wisconsin economist, John R. Commons, all of whom lent their prestige to efforts to encourage reform. Florence Kelley's National Consumers' League was one of the most militant of these associations. Another, the Women's Trade Union League, fought long and hard against exploitation of industrial workers. The American Association for Labor Legislation, headed throughout its existence by John B. Andrews, grew from about two hundred members in 1906 to more than three thousand in 1919. Through writing and lobbying, it helped bring about the adoption of rudimentary work-men's compensation laws in many states. Andrews had stud-ied and collaborated with John R. Commons, and he exerted great influence on many other reform groups.[2]

By 1912, former Republican President Theodore Roosevelt, a great reformer, had become disillusioned with the policies of his successor, William Howard Taft. Although Roosevelt had strongly supported Taft to follow him in office, his former friend's complacency and unwillingness to pursue reform of-fended him profoundly. Roosevelt therefore attempted to re-gain the Republican nomination from Taft in 1912. The Re-publican leaders found Taft's policies to be considerably more congenial than those that the uncontrollable Roosevelt might adopt and renominated the President. Roosevelt then launched a third-party candidacy as the candidate of the "Bull Moose" Progressives, a new party that included a call for so-cial insurance in its platform. Although Roosevelt's second-place finish was uniquely strong in the twentieth century for a minor party's candidate, his defeat ensured that social insur-ance was unlikely to be considered seriously for some time.

Shortly thereafter, I. M. Rubinow, a physician turned econo-mist and statistician, set forth the theoretical justification for what came to be the Social Security Act in his classic work of 1913, *Social Insurance*. He had been with the U.S. Bureau of Labor and was a lecturer on social insurance at the New York School of Philanthropy. He traced the background of social in-surance in Europe and described the various programs then in existence.

With publication of this book, Rubinow became the leading authority on social insurance in the United States. Until his death shortly after the passage of the Social Security Act—which owed much to his pioneering and continuing efforts—he remained one of the foremost of a small group of American experts in the field.

Rubinow refuted the prevailing argument that America's high wages eliminated the need for social insurance. Wages, he wrote, were not sufficiently high to yield a continuous surplus. An annual surplus in income, which would make it possible to save anything for retirement or disability, was in fact quite rare for a worker.[3] It required the crisis of the Great Depression finally to force recognition of Rubinow's point.

During the rise of the progressive movement, social reformers developed a spirit of cooperation with government officials at all levels. The reformers tended to consider Theodore Roosevelt's defeat in his third-party run to regain the presidency in 1912 to be a blow to their cause. Nevertheless, the cooperation continued to some degree under the Wilson administration until World War I destroyed it by redirecting popular concerns and associating many reform measures with "pro-German" sympathies. It was impossible to restore the relationship during the era of "normalcy" after the war. The mood of the 1920s was apathetic and largely unconcerned with social justice. It was hardly conducive to reform measures.[4]

The first brief flurry of activity in support of governmental health insurance in the United States had spanned the war years. In 1912, the American Association for Labor Legislation formed the country's first Committee on Social Insurance. In 1913, the association sponsored a national conference on social security. The conference led to the drafting of a model social insurance bill, including health insurance provisions, for introduction into state legislatures. The Committee on Social Insurance appointed a subcommittee in 1914 specifically to prepare the bill, and the subcommittee completed its task in 1915. In the same year, the American Medical Association also displayed interest in compulsory government health insurance and formed its own Social Insurance Committee. Three of its members, Alexander Lambert, I. M. Rubinow, and S. S. Goldwater, all physicians, were members of the committee formed earlier by the American Association for Labor Legislation. The AMA and the AALL were prepared to cooperate upon the medical issues involved, but the cooperation was brief. By 1918, serious opposition had arisen within the AMA, and many insurance companies and pharmaceutical houses had also begun to work against the program.[5]

The model social insurance bill was introduced into the New York legislature in 1916, 1917, and 1918. During those years, legislatures from many states established commissions to investigate the issues involved, the strongest ones being in New York and California. Rubinow published a new book in 1916, *Standards of Health Insurance*, that furthered the movement. In 1919, the bill providing for health insurance passed the New York Senate, but even with support from Governor Al Smith, it failed in the assembly's Rules Committee. By 1920, health insurance had ceased to be a serious political issue in the United States, and the AMA went on record with a policy of strenuous opposition that lasted for decades.

In August 1921, during the brief postwar depression that had begun in 1920, President Warren G. Harding called a Conference on Unemployment. The conference accomplished little, since improving economic conditions had lessened the pressure on the participants. Their attitude was indicated by comments from the chair of the conference's Subcommittee on Public Works, Otto T. Mallery. Reformers had attacked the conference for not considering unemployment insurance. Mallery retorted that if the conference had considered such an untried measure that had no public support, it would have jeopardized serious consideration of other issues.

The depression had occasioned some talk of public works and centralized employment services, but the rapid recovery quickly stifled such notions. Likewise, when Paul H. Douglas, University of Chicago economist and future U. S. senator, published his *Wages and the Family* in 1925, his suggestion that America attempt a program providing something similar to the family allowances already widely prevalent in Europe aroused little interest.[6] In many instances, proposals for social security legislation of any sort brought expressions of horror.

A Massachusetts study branded ideas for old-age pensions as a "counsel of despair" and said that "if such a scheme be defensible or excusable in this country, then the whole economic and social system is a failure."[7]

Regardless of the prevailing apathy, there were a few faint sparks of social reform sentiment that remained even in the 1920s. The Fraternal Order of Eagles and the American Association for Labor Legislation jointly proposed that states adopt old-age pension plans, and they drafted a model bill for state legislatures to consider.[8] Paul Douglas wrote that there were "certain undercurrents of public opinion which were beginning to change on the subject of old-age pensions" even before the Great Depression. He noted that eight states—Colorado, Kentucky, Maryland, Montana, Minnesota, Nevada, Utah, and Wisconsin—passed acts enabling counties to set up programs and that Wisconsin and Minnesota even provided aid to those counties that did so. In 1929, California and Wisconsin became the first states to adopt mandatory acts. New York and Massachusetts followed in 1930. Colorado (replacing the original act), Delaware, Idaho, New Jersey, and New Hampshire followed in 1931, to be joined in 1933 by Arizona, Indiana, Maine, Michigan, Nebraska, North Dakota, Ohio, Oregon, Pennsylvania, and Washington. By the middle of 1934, twenty-eight states plus the Territories of Alaska and Hawaii had passed old-age pension acts, all but five of them mandatory.[9] These acts had passed despite continued distaste for governmental activity, because the situation had become so extreme that the legislatures recognized that something had to be done.

Although there were no national statistics, and few local governments maintained accurate or adequate information, danger signals existed in the 1920s. Some observers recognized them. Settlement workers, especially, were likely to sense something amiss. Residents at the Chicago Commons, for example, in 1928 began to report increasing unemployment. Similar reports came from other settlements. Rubinow noted in 1926 that, despite rising wages, there was a rising social service caseload occasioned by increasing unemployment. He called for social workers to turn from their preoccupation with "bad physical heredity, inadequate personality, lack of initiative, psychoses and neuroses, and constitutional inferiority. . . and take up the cause of social insurance." Few paid heed.[10]

One who did was Abraham Epstein, the research director for the Pennsylvania Old Age Pension Commission. In 1927 he was instrumental in forming a new organization, the American Association for Old Age Security. Through his lobbying activities and publications, Epstein soon joined Douglas and Rubinow as the most prominent advocates of social insurance in the United States. In 1928, the same year that *Harper's Magazine* rejected one of his articles because they sensed in it a "Bolshevik air," Epstein began to notice somewhat more enthusiasm. Not only were more counties adopting pension programs, but his audiences were beginning to increase. In 1931—at the depth of the misery occasioned by the Great Depression—his organization was suddenly influential.[11] In 1933, he changed its name to the American Association for Social Security to reflect the group's broadened interests.

Early in the 1930s, three books added considerable impetus to the social insurance movement: Paul Douglas's *The Problem of Unemployment* (1931), Epstein's *Insecurity: A Challenge to America* (1933; revised 1936), and Rubinow's *Quest for Security* (1934). Epstein wrote of social insurance as carrying the principle of private insurance "to its logical limit."[12] Rubinow's *Quest* was an extension of his 1913 work, *Social Insurance*, the first comprehensive treatment of the subject in the United States. *Quest* dealt with what Rubinow saw as the confused, illogical state of mind of most Americans on the subject of "relief" (now we can substitute the word "welfare"). He asked why accepting assistance should be considered a disgrace, when no one minds taking advantage of free concerts, regardless of whether they are financed by some patron of the arts or by the city—which is government. He said that social workers who administered relief occasionally saw clients who possessed such pride that they refused material assistance. In such situations, he noted, the social workers used strong arguments to break down the client's "dignity" (for example, "Why should your family suffer because of your pride?") but secretly admired it. He cited studies showing that a "respectable non-pauperized family" typically endured from six to eight months of unemployment before applying for relief of any sort.[13]

Despite complaints today about a "welfare culture," many potential welfare recipients continue to refuse to apply for benefits from means-tested programs. This point shone clearly through Martha Derthick's cautious language, for example, when she wrote that analyses of Supplemental Security Income (SSI), a means-tested program for the poor, "in operation have consistently estimated the rate of participation among the elderly at 50–60 percent of those who are eligible. It seems possible that many of the aged, at least, continue to be deterred by the stigma attached to means-tested assistance."[14]

Fortunately, there is no stigma attached to Social Security because its benefits are perceived to be earned. It also reduces the need for other forms of assistance. The Social Security system was a response to the need for government action in a society that remained suspicious of government, and its designers crafted it to preserve individual dignity. The legislation that brought it forth was the culmination of the story that this chapter tells. In the next chapter we will turn to that legislation, the Social Security Act of 1935.

3

FDR's Plan and
Its Enemies
Emerge

All hesitation about social insurance ended when Franklin D. Roosevelt became president in 1933. FDR was a distant cousin of Theodore Roosevelt. Although TR was a Republican and FDR a Democrat, there was much in FDR's New Deal that built on the groundwork that TR laid down during the Progressive period, both during his time as president and subsequently. As I mentioned in Chapter 2, in TR's "Bull Moose" campaign of 1912, when he attempted unsuccessfully to regain the presidency, his platform proposed a comprehensive system of social insurance.

During the New Deal, two of the federal officials who were to be most influential in the government's attempts to provide social security were Harry Hopkins (the federal emergency relief administrator) and Secretary of Labor Frances Perkins (the first woman to serve in the cabinet). Both had long experience in social reform movements, the settlement houses, and the field of social work. Perkins had been with Jane Addams at Hull House, had studied economics under Simon Patton (the University of Pennsylvania economist who was known as an advocate of government economic planning), had been executive secretary of the Consumers' League in New York, and had long been within the inner circle of the social work profession.[1] She had also traveled to England in 1931 at the request of Roosevelt, then governor of New York, to study the British system of unemployment insurance.[2] Hopkins had worked at Christodora House, a settlement in New York, and was a past president of the American Association of Social Workers.[3]

On 29 June 1934, the president issued Executive Order 6757 creating the Committee on Economic Security composed of the secretary of labor (chair), the secretary of the treasury, the attorney general, the secretary of agriculture, and the federal emergency relief administrator. The previous day the attorney general had ruled that the National Industrial Recovery Act had empowered the president to create such a committee. The committee's report, dated 15 January 1935, contained the outline of what was to become the Social Security system. The report incorporated some of the principles of private insurance, or an "insurance company model," into the provisions for old-age benefits.

The committee's recommendations were introduced into Congress in January by Representatives David J. Lewis (D.–Md.) and Robert L. Doughton (D.–N.C.) in the House, and Senator Robert F. Wagner (D.–N.Y.) in the Senate. Although Representative Doughton, who chaired the Ways and Means Committee, had not previously been noted for support of social insurance, his own bill (H.R. 4120) took precedence in the House. At this stage it was called the Economic Security Bill, but the Ways and Means Committee rewrote it extensively and substituted its own bill (H. R. 7260). Thereafter it was referred to as the Social Security Bill. It was this bill that the House passed and sent to the Senate Finance Committee, which reported it (and not the Wagner Bill) to the Senate for passage.[4]

The example of the private insurance company was certainly not the only argument used by proponents of the Social Security Bill, and applied to only one of its benefits. Even so, it was among their most forceful arguments and seemed to have the greatest appeal to the public. The idea of incorporating the principles of private insurance, such as "premiums," certain provisions of individual equity, and the like, into a social insurance system were not unique to the United States, but they were so in keeping with American experience and preferences that apparently no one even seriously proposed an alternative to the insurance-company model. That model, of course, applied only to the general program, that for old-age benefits. Those that were limited to special categories (such as aid to the blind, or aid to dependent children) or that involved means tests were unaffected by the notion of insurance. A program applicable to the general population, however, seemed to require a rationalization—"old age" in this sense is not a special category, since the population generally can anticipate becoming elderly.

Congress seemed to be even more insistent upon the insurance-company model for this program than were the original planners. Both the administration and the Congress were anxious to avoid contributions to old-age benefits from general revenues, as the original draft had contemplated. Accordingly, the tax rates finally voted to finance the program were higher than those recommended in the report of the Committee on Economic Security.[5]

Many prominent members of both parties supported the Social Security Act or similar programs, but Republicans as a group tended to be more reluctant to support such an innovative measure. The final vote in the House was 372 in favor (288 Democrats, 77 Republicans, 6 Progressives, and 1 Farmer-Labor), and 33 opposed (13 Democrats, 18 Republicans, and 2 Farmer-Labor). In the Senate the final vote was 77 in favor (60 Democrats, 15 Republicans, 1 Progressive, and 1 Farmer-Labor), and 6 (1 Democrat and 5 Republicans) opposed—but the Republicans just prior to the final tally voted 12 to 8 to eliminate old-age insurance.[6]

President Franklin D. Roosevelt signed the act into law on 14 August 1935. Payroll taxes began in 1937. That same year the Supreme Court approved the Social Security Act and declared it to be constitutional.

The act originally provided for administration by a Social Security Board, which began operation in 1936. The board was later abolished by the creation of a Social Security Administration within a Federal Security Agency during the Truman administration. The FSA itself was transformed into the Department of Health, Education, and Welfare, during the Eisenhower administration. DHEW became the Department of Health and Human Services under President Carter, when education was stripped off to become the Department of Education. Because of its enormous size, the Social Security Administration under President Clinton came full circle and once again became an independent agency, reporting directly to the president.

The contributory program of old-age insurance was purely federal, and it has remained so. The act also established other kinds of protections besides old-age insurance, and these generally involve federal-state cooperation. Among its innovations were unemployment benefits and various other federal-state programs to aid specific groups.

Under the original act, for example, the old-age assistance provision made possible pensions for the elderly poor; this provision has been expanded into Supplemental Security Income (SSI), a means-tested program. Assistance to poor children took the form of Aid to Dependent Children (ADC), also means tested, which became Aid to Families with Dependent Children (AFDC). This program was vastly curtailed under the Clinton administration, becoming Temporary Assistance to Needy Families (TANF). Critics argue that it has been virtually eliminated. Responding to public outrage regarding "welfare," President Clinton worked closely with a Republican Congress to tighten requirements for benefits and to make them available only for a restricted period during the lifetime of any person.

Other sections of the Social Security Act set up grants to the states to assist in providing services for the blind or dis-

abled, for vocational rehabilitation, and for public health services. The tendency of the public, of course, is to think only
of old-age insurance, the contributory federal program, when
thinking of "Social Security." The better informed may also
include survivors' and disability insurance, along with
Medicare, but rarely if ever does the term include the other
programs.

The Reaction: Politics, Parties, and the Public

The results of the 1936 elections returning Franklin D. Roosevelt to power were devastating to the Republican Party.
FDR was one of only four presidents in the twentieth century
to reach 60 percent of the popular vote. Warren Harding in
1920, Lyndon Johnson in 1964, and Richard Nixon in 1972
were the others. That only 60 percent constitutes a landslide
is an indication of how broad the split in American political
opinion is. To be sure, there tends to be an American consen-
sus on many fundamentals of the political system—probably
as great as that existing in any Western democracy. Nevertheless, there is a huge disagreement on ways in which to implement those fundamentals, as the continuing debate over Social Security illustrates. Even when a major party goes down
to a crushing defeat, as the Republicans did in 1936, it remains a large minority and one that commands a considerable
following.

The party platforms for that year are illuminating. As was
to have been expected, the Social Security Act was a major
subject of debate in the campaign. Various minor parties
called for additional programs to assist those in need.

The Prohibition Party claimed in its platform that it had
been the very first party to endorse the idea of old-age pensions, and it called for additional governmental aid to the elderly and the disabled.[7] Father Charles Coughlin, an early radio demagogue noted for his anti-Semitic diatribes, had

established his Union Party, which also called for security for the aged. His platform said that they had been "victimized and exploited by an unjust economic system which has so concentrated wealth in the hands of a few that it has impoverished great masses of our people." The Socialist Party called for immediate appropriation of six billion dollars for relief to the unemployed for the coming year. To this they added a call for unemployment insurance, old-age pensions for all over sixty—to be financed through income and inheritance taxes as in the Frazier-Lundeen Bill—and health care for all to be provided "as a social duty, not as a private or public charity." The platform of the Communist Party contained an entire section entitled "Provide Unemployment Insurance, Old Age Pensions, and Social Security for All." The Communists defined social security in a broad sense, advocating the addition of health and maternity benefits.

The Democrats, of course, boasted of the Social Security Act. They described in glowing terms the measures that it provided and pledged to use it as a base to erect a "structure of economic security" for everyone.

The official platform of the Republican Party, on the other hand, declared that real security would be possible only when the country's productive capacity was sufficient to provide it. To attain that goal, it said, Republicans looked "to the energy, self-reliance and character" of the people, and to the system of free enterprise. Following this, however, their platform proposed a system for old-age security based upon four parts: First a pay-as-you-go system requiring each generation to support the aged and to determine "what is just and adequate"; second, a supplementary payment sufficient to provide income large enough to protect all American citizens over sixty-five from want; third, graduated payments to states and territories for cooperative financing of security programs that have met "simple and general minimum standards"; and fourth, "a direct tax widely distributed" to finance the federal part of the program. They would require contributions from all, since all

would be benefited. The Republicans said that the system under the Social Security Act would be too complicated to be administered and charged that the tax burden would be too great
and that the program would benefit too few people.[8]

Many supporters of social insurance who had hoped for
something more extensive than the Social Security Act
greeted the Republican proposals warmly. An editorial in *The
Nation* of 24 June 1936, for example, said that although "a direct tax widely distributed" sounded suspiciously as if it
meant a sales tax, the social insurance plank of the Republican platform was better than the plans of the Democrats because it called for revenue to support the program to be de-
rived from general taxation.

Evelyn M. Burns, then an economist at Columbia University and vice president of the American Association for Social
Welfare, replied with a letter to the editor that cut through the
misunderstandings and fuzzy conclusions that so often mark
comments on Social Security. She was "very surprised" when
she read the editorial, her letter of 11 July said, because the
Republican platform did not provide at all for social insurance
as the phrase was generally understood. She pointed out that
the platform did not mention benefits as a matter of right,
only on the basis of need.

Much rhetoric on Social Security since around 1980 is
phrased subtly to give the impression that it supports the system but nevertheless remains based on the same idea. The
proposals by Peter Peterson and the Concord Coalition are the
most widely publicized examples. They would "strengthen"
Social Security by what Peterson calls "affluence testing,"
which would deny benefits to all but the needy while still requiring all workers to pay into the system.

Burns agreed that means-tested programs had a place in a
broad social security scheme, but that they were "comple-
mentary." Such provisions had already been established by
the Social Security Act as old-age assistance. She added that
the Social Security plan, regardless of the merits of its financ-

ing, at least gave something in return to the contributor. The Republican plan, she said, would tax everyone but pay benefits only to those who subjected themselves to a means test. Further, as a cooperative program with the states, it would provide no benefits at all in states that elected not to participate.

The editors retreated hastily. They had not meant to contrast the "illiberal Republican plank with the Social Security Act," they said, "but with the party's complete silence on the subject in 1932." They agreed with Burns's statements, they said, and had written their editorial "largely because of the reactionary nature of the platform as a whole." As is often the case, the liberal tendency to attempt to be "objective" and fair to the opposition led them to undermine their own case. Their explanation was not only lame but inaccurate. Moreover, they could as easily have contrasted the 1936 Democratic platform with that of 1932, when it also had remained silent on the subject. The only parties that had specifically advocated social insurance in their 1932 platforms were the Socialist and the Farmer-Labor Parties. Each had supported social insurance for many years, the Farmer-Labor Party since 1920, and the Socialists in every presidential campaign since 1900.

The closest the idea had come to acceptance by a major party before Franklin D. Roosevelt was the inclusion mentioned above in Theodore Roosevelt's 1912 Bull Moose Progressive platform. Neither Republicans nor Democrats had dealt with it in their platform until 1936, a year after passage of the Social Security Act. The only earlier mention of a related subject by the Democrats appears to have been in their platform of 1916, in which they supported a law providing for "the retirement of superannuated and disabled civil servants" so that a "higher standard of efficiency may be maintained."

The Republicans' record was similar. Their only mention of a related subject before 1936 seems to have been in their 1924 platform, in which they called for the creation of a cabinet

post of education and relief to coordinate the various depart-
ments administering the federal government's "numerous and
important" welfare activities. This proposal is ironic in view
of the calls by Ronald Reagan and numerous other Republicans since his presidency to eliminate the Department of Education.

There was nothing ambivalent about the public reaction,
which was enthusiastic about the program. So great was the
public enthusiasm that it invested Social Security with an effective shield against most criticism from elected officials.
That shield made certain that Republicans as well as Democrats would officially accept Social Security's general principle that the welfare of the people was a legitimate concern of
the government and that government had an obligation to assist in ensuring that welfare. Official Republican criticism of
the Social Security Act did not extend to criticism of the principles of Social Security.

Their 1936 presidential candidate, Governor Alf Landon of
Kansas, remarked in a radio address on 7 May, "I'm for it.
Every big industrial nation has had to move in that direction.
In America we could once handle the problem pretty well by
depending on individual thrift, family aid, local taxation and
private contributions. These still have their place and a vital
place it is." He also mentioned the pension systems of some
of the more progressive business concerns but said that it was
now necessary for the government "to take a hand." Revers-
ing cause and effect, he indicated that the administration's
program did increase public attention to the problem (as
though the public had not known the problems people were
facing) but that it was "complicated legislation the Administration rushed through in characteristic fashion."[9]

The recognition of Social Security's popularity dampened
criticism from politicians, but it did not completely protect
the system from attack. The first concerted effort came in the
form of notices that many employers nationwide included in
their employees' pay envelopes. During the 1936 campaign,

workers throughout the country discovered notices with their pay that charged that Social Security was nothing but a scheme to raise taxes. The notices typically failed even to mention that the program involved benefits or that the employer was to pay half of the tax. Joseph P. Kennedy, who then headed the Securities and Exchange Commission—and was certainly anything but a radical—said that the pay-envelope campaign was grossly unfair and false and that it attempted to "create the impression that giving old age insurance at half-price to the worker is an unfair tax on the worker."[10]

President Roosevelt gave an address in Madison Square Garden on 31 October in which he attacked the employers engaging in the pay-envelope campaign, calling them deceitful for neglecting to tell the complete story. He charged that they were attempting to mislead their workers into voting against him. Social Security provided two "policies," he said, unemployment insurance to be paid for by the employer, and the old-age program paid for jointly by the employer and the employee. On the second of November, an editorial in the *New York Herald Tribune* called the President's speech "bitter and defiant."

Sociologists who were studying Muncie, Indiana, at the time found that "Landon and higher wages" was the theme of the attack there.[11] Pay envelopes from Muncie factories included stuffers critical of New Deal programs. They emphasized the deductions from workers' pay and charged that Social Security would make raises impossible. They did not mention benefits, but did charge that the system would soon collapse.

Some of the most bitter criticism of Roosevelt and the New Deal came from the Hearst newspapers. Discussing Landon's views on social insurance, for example, an editorial in late May said:

He is careful to imply that it . . . must be along AMERICAN lines, and not be a detail in a general scheme such as this Administration has put forth, to reduce millions of Americans to the condition of STATE PARASITES. In fact, one great fault of Mr. Roosevelt is that he has, by his extreme and extravagant methods, discredited all progressive ideas. Governor Landon, however, indicates that no social security legislation based on COLLECTIVIST DELUSIONS or that is plainly UNCONSTITUTIONAL will receive his assent.[12]

In a speech at Syracuse in September 1936, the president defended the Social Security Act against such attacks and denied that it was "radical and alien."[13] All the while, Governor Landon was working to bring his state under the provisions of the act. He called the Kansas Legislature into a special session on 7 July 1936 to begin work on an amendment to the state's constitution that would permit it to participate.

The most severe criticisms came from groups with special interests. Henry Ford issued a statement during the campaign that was typical of much of this criticism:

Under some social security systems abroad a man cannot quit his job, or apply for another, or leave town and go to another even to get a better job because that would break the "economic plan." Such a restriction of liberty will be almost a necessity in this country too if the present Social Security Act works to its natural conclusions.[14]

At the same time the United States Chamber of Commerce took a somewhat more moderate viewpoint and expressed it in a "Statement of Principles" said to represent the opinions of its 1,400 member organizations, including some 700,000 members. Of Social Security, the Chamber said:

Business would ignore its gravest responsibility if it failed to provide the greatest possible degree of economic security to the individual. The attainment of this end so necessary to the furtherance of American ideals will require not only the maintenance of high wages but likewise a constructive solution to the complex problem of security to the individual when he or she has outlived capacity to earn a comfortable living. Here again interference by government in attempts to reduce the whole complex problem to one of legislative formulae can only postpone the final solution by making it more difficult for business to assume its own obligations in the matter.[15]

Some three years after FDR's landslide victory, Professor Raymond Pearl of Johns Hopkins University, then president of the American Statistical Association, made some remarks that should still give us food for thought today. They illustrate that the opposition had not been extinguished, but more important, they reveal just how extreme was some of the criticism. Dr. Pearl—who was himself sixty years of age at the time—suggested that, by their advocacy of old-age pension "nostrums," the aged might be proving themselves too foolish to be allowed the privilege of voting. He said that the elderly together with the young "are ganging up on the half of the population that does the work." The demands of the young had decreased somewhat, he conceded, but the increase in the proportion of persons who have "finished whatever biological justification there ever was for existence" constituted a social problem of the first magnitude.[16]

Most comments of this kind today employ somewhat more tactful rhetoric, but it would be a grave mistake to conclude that this kind of attitude no longer exists. More than hints of it appear in the comments of some of the more candid opponents of social welfare when they discuss the baby boomers and issue their dire forecasts for Social Security—especially if the discussions are off the record.

Several commentators in the early years did praise the purposes of the Social Security Act even while criticizing its provisions. An editorial in *Collier's* said that "few have quarreled with the broad purposes underlying the Social Security Act. On the other hand many of the most experienced and sincere advocates of social insurance are aghast at some of the provisions. . . ."[17] *Collier's* neither identified these "experienced and sincere advocates" nor specified which of the act's provisions so perturbed its editor. The chairman of the board of Chase National Bank, Winthrop W. Aldrich, echoed the sentiments in *Collier's*. Many people were sympathetic to Social Security's intent, he said, but its form created a "grave menace to the future security of the country as a whole and to the security of the very people it is designed to protect."[18]

Opposition was not limited to words: there were lawsuits as well. For example, a stockholder in the Union Elastic Co. of Easthampton, Dean A. Fales, filed a suit asking the court to declare the Social Security Act void. He believed that it would reduce the value of his shares and constituted an illegal seizure of property.[19]

The pervasive criticism died quickly because of its futility—the public obviously supported Social Security strongly. Public opinion polling was in its infancy, but early polls were unanimous in identifying powerful public support for the program. Paul Douglas marveled at the abrupt change. Before the Great Depression, he wrote, public opinion held overwhelmingly that "American citizens could in the main provide for their old age by individual savings."[20] In a series of Gallup polls taken from December, 1935, to November, 1939, the American Institute of Public Opinion revealed that no fewer than 89 percent of those interviewed said that they were in favor of "government old age pensions for needy persons," and 91 percent indicated approval in the July 1941 poll that even deleted the phrase "for needy persons."[21]

One of the gravest concerns that those fearing the effects of Social Security expressed had to do with the assignment of identification numbers. The Social Security Act emerged when the threat from totalitarian systems was concrete and immediate, not merely potential. Some critics were terrified that the Social Security number would become the identifier that permitted government to keep track of each citizen and delve deeply into his or her private life. In response, Social Security officials assured the public that they would maintain vigilance against the misuse of the numbers. For the most part, they restricted their use completely to purposes of the Social Security system. Even after President Roosevelt's Executive Order 9397 in 1943 ordered all agencies of the federal government to use the Social Security number when creating new identification systems for people, Social Security's administrators continued to work diligently to demonstrate that the early fears had been groundless.

In the 1950s, whenever other government agencies sought to use Social Security records for law-enforcement purposes—perhaps to trace someone, the Social Security Administration adamantly refused. It continued to hold its files confidential. SSA folklore had it that occasionally the agency would discover and discharge an infiltrator, a government agent perhaps from the FBI, who had gained employment undercover to work in its files. A breach occurred in 1975 when legislation permitted the use of Social Security records to help locate absent fathers who were not paying child support as ordered to children who were receiving welfare payments. The justification was that such use of the records was for Social Security purposes, because payments to dependent children and their families came under a program that the Social Security Act created.

The barrier had already begun to crumble in 1961, when the former Civil Service Commission adopted the Social Security number as the official Federal employee identifier, and legislation required each taxpayer to report his or her number on tax returns. The Internal Revenue Service the following year converted it into a federal identification number, to be used on tax returns and other records. In 1967 the Department of Defense substituted the Social Security number for the former service numbers as personal identifiers of military personnel. 1970 legislation required banks and other financial institutions to obtain the Social Security numbers of all customers and to report—by the number—any transaction exceeding $10,000.

Now the use of the number is virtually universal and ties together a vast array of information having nothing to do with Social Security. Tax returns, records regarding health, banking, driver's licenses, military records, pilot's licenses, and almost every conceivable kind of data—public and private, local and state as well as national—that can be recorded can now be uncovered through the use of what was previously the sacrosanct Social Security number. All the while, legislation continues to proclaim that there is to be no "universal identification number" in the United States.

Perhaps not, but the early critics were at least close to being correct in their predictions that the numbers would become all-purpose identifiers, despite the assurances of the supporters that it would not happen. Happily, though, the critics' worst fears have not been realized. For a variety of reasons, including some protective legislation, the data-driven police state that they assumed would follow has not materialized—at least not yet. We can hope that it will not and should exercise vigilance to ensure that it does not.

There is little controversy regarding the Social Security number any longer. The world is so dominated by records and files that we have come to accept as necessary some form of identifier—and that number is as good as any other for the purpose. The enormous good that Social Security accomplishes overshadows concerns about its records. Far from engendering the intergenerational conflict that some of its opponents allege, it is one program that binds Americans—regardless of generation—together, benefiting them all and ensuring that all contribute to their country's well-being.

The next chapter will examine the way in which Social Security has expanded through the years, how the emphasis of the program has shifted, and how—despite fierce opposition—Medicare came to be.

4

From Mrs. Fuller's First Check

The original Social Security Act of 1935 provided for a rebate to those who had paid taxes but did not qualify for benefits. The act did not provide for benefits to be paid until the first of January, 1942, but amendments in 1939 revised the benefit formula, and changed the date of first benefit payments to 31 January 1940. The first check ($22.54) went to a retired legal secretary from Vermont, Ida Mae Fuller, who lived for another 35 years. She died at the age of 100.

The original provisions—designed for strict individual equity—were never in force. The 1939 amendments added benefits for wives and for widows and children of deceased workers, thus incorporating an emphasis upon the family. (As a result of the 1977 *Goldfarb* decision, husbands and widowers became eligible for benefits on the same basis as wives and widows.) This family emphasis, coupled with the elimination of the rebate, greatly weakened the principle of individual equity. From that point on, married workers, especially those with children, have received much more for their contributions than childless or unmarried workers. The 1939 amendments also added an advantage for low-income and short-term workers.

The legislation was a striking departure from tradition for Americans, but it provided considerably less than many programs elsewhere. Germany, for example, the country that had pioneered social insurance in the 1880s, had expanded its system to cover the disabled some two decades before America's Social Security Act. Although the American program has grown steadily both in terms of the number of people covered and the range of benefits offered, it continues to lag behind those in other industrial countries.

The first expansion following the great revisions of 1939 came with the 1950 amendments, which added coverage for the self-employed (farmers and certain professionals, such as ministers and physicians, remained uncovered). Domestic and farm workers also came under coverage. The amendments also raised the tax rate to 1.5 percent and increased the taxable wage base to $3,600. Amendments in 1952 brought self-employed farmers under coverage and provided voluntary coverage to ministers and certain other professionals.

In 1956, during the Eisenhower administration, Congress added a huge benefit, coverage for disability. The legislation also made provisions for women to retire early, at sixty-two, if they chose to do so with reduced benefits. The same amendments brought coverage to self-employed dentists, lawyers, optometrists, osteopaths (D.O.s), and veterinarians. In 1958, Congress again increased benefits, raising the taxable wage base to $4,800 and including benefits for eligible dependents of disability beneficiaries. As of 1959, the tax rate went up to 2.5 percent. Originally, disability benefits were available only to those aged fifty or older. In 1960 amendments removed the age restriction. In 1961, men became eligible to retire early at sixty-two along with women. Beginning in 1962, the tax again increased, this time to 3.125 percent.

The largest addition of benefits came during the Johnson administration in 1965 with the addition of Medicare. It was a long and difficult battle. Congress approved the program only after years of acrimonious controversy, with the American Medical Association being the most vigorous and bitter opponent. Branding Medicare "socialized medicine," the AMA succeeded in delaying the program for decades. The long delay led increasing numbers of the elderly to go without necessary care, to obtain care only by sacrificing self-respect and seeking charity, or to find themselves with crushing bills that they could not pay.

As early as 1920, the governing body of the American Medical Association, its House of Delegates, met to solidify its strenuous opposition to government assistance in meeting citizens' health expenses. The following resolution was the result of this New Orleans meeting:

> *Resolved*, that the American Medical Association declares its opposition to the institution of any plan embodying the system of compulsory contributory insurance against illness, or any other plan of compulsory insurance which provides for medical service to be rendered contributors or their dependents, provided, controlled or regulated by any state or the federal government.

The AMA's official history, published in 1947, declared that this resolution was the official policy of the association and had remained so since 1920.[1] Although the association's opposition was strong and consistent and had begun early, the issue in fact lay dormant for another decade after 1920, until the Committee on the Costs of Medical Care released its majority report in 1932. Then the subject again emerged as a serious political issue, and discussions of social insurance included the possibility that it might be incorporated as part of the system. President Roosevelt decided against proposing health care as a part of Social Security, because he feared that organized medicine's powerful opposition might defeat the entire program.

In 1939, Senator Robert F. Wagner of New York introduced a proposal to establish a national health program providing grants to the states, which were to develop health plans conforming to federal standards. There had been several related bills previously, but this was the first to receive serious attention. The subcommittee examining the bill issued a favorable interim report, the AMA produced twenty-two arguments against it, and there was no further action at the time.[2] The year 1943 saw the introduction of the first of a series of Wagner-Murray-Dingell Bills that would have established a national system of hospitals and medical benefits, financed by a payroll tax on employees and employers. It would have provided the patient with free choice of participating physicians and authorized the surgeon general of the Public Health Service to set fee schedules and regulate the number of patients each physician would treat. The reaction from organized medicine was immediate and hostile. The National Physicians Committee (see below) charged that "the processes proposed and the mechanisms indicated are designed to act as the catalyst in transforming a rapidly expanding Federal bureaucracy into an all powerful totalitarian state control. Human rights as opposed to slavery is the issue."[3] The bill died in committee.

A similar fate lay in store for the second Wagner-Murray-Dingell Bill in 1945, even though it had strong support from the Truman administration. The Republican Eightieth Congress considered a revised Wagner-Murray-Dingell Bill in 1947. Both this and the 1945 version provided for state administration of a federal program. Both failed.

The last major Truman administration health bill was that of 1949. This bill, similar to the Wagner-Murray-Dingell Bill of 1947, was based upon the Federal Security Agency's report to the president, *The Nation's Health, A Ten-Year Program*, by Oscar Ewing. During the 1948 campaign, the president had strongly urged the adoption of the principles of the Ewing report. Truman's election victory heightened anxiety for many members of the AMA. There had also been Republican alternatives to the Wagner-Murray-Dingell proposals. Senator Robert A. Taft of Ohio had sponsored a series of bills in 1946, 1947, and 1949 calling for state-operated programs of aid to those unable to pay for health care. The AMA did not attack

Taft's proposals but failed to support them because of concerns about lay administrators at local levels.[4]

When the AMA did employ its propaganda machinery, it did so vigorously. Its advertising tended to link policies it opposed with socialism and communism. It even tried to tie such policies specifically to the Soviet Union. During the 1940s, the association developed a consistent, coherent pattern of strategic attack. From 1939 to 1948, it expressed its opposition through a National Physicians Committee for the Extension of Medical Service (NPC), which it apparently brought into existence in response to the Wagner Bill of 1939. Although the AMA denied any connection with NPC, AMA members headed it, and AMA fundraising mechanisms supported it. Both the profession and the public considered the NPC to be the official voice for the AMA. Presumably the rationale for the arrangement was fear that the AMA's charter as a non-profit organization would prevent it from any extensive direct lobbying. Such fears seemed to lessen as the years passed, if AMA activities during subsequent years are any indication. For many of those years the AMA was among the most active of all lobbying groups and was at or near the top in the amount of spending to influence legislation. During the NPC's existence, however, the association confined its "official" activities of opposition to speeches, editorials, legislative testimony, and resolutions by its House of Delegates.

The NPC worked through physicians' offices to distribute a huge number of pamphlets and other printed material concerning governmental health insurance. By 1948, however, its influence had waned, owing to a growing reaction against some of its propaganda tactics and a public distaste for some of the right-wing extremist groups with which it had become associated.[5] Even before then, the AMA had taken some steps to cleanse its reputation. In 1946 it hired a special public relations counsel for the purpose. Then, in 1949, Dr. Morris Fishbein, who had been intimately involved in the association's opposition to health insurance, specifically with much of the extreme language that had characterized the AMA's political activities since the 1930s, retired as editor of the *Journal of the American Medical Association*, (*JAMA*). He had received considerable criticism from within the profession as having been largely responsible for much of the tarnish on organized medicine's professional image. Although his successors generally adopted less vitriolic language, observers who hoped for more moderate policies were disappointed.

With Truman's 1948 victory, the AMA began extensive efforts to launch strong and positive programs of opposition to governmental health insurance and to appeal to the citizenry for support. With great haste the House of Delegates levied an assessment of twenty-five dollars on each member to build a $3.5 million "political war chest to fight socialized medicine." It planned a "National Education Campaign," consisting of a barrage of advertisements, to "educate" the American people, and it employed the public relations firm of Whitaker and Baxter to direct the campaign.

Initially there was opposition within the association to the assessment, but the National Education Campaign successfully sold the idea to the membership. Virtually all members displayed posters and distributed pamphlets to patients. Physicians and their wives (women physicians were rare in those days) distributed some twenty million pamphlets in the first year. Instructions to wives called for them to "tuck pamphlets into all . . . personal correspondence—even invitations to dinner parties"—but to avoid debates. Additionally, the personal physicians of members of Congress urged their powerfully placed patients to support AMA views. Cooperating with the physicians were (among others) insurance agents and companies, dentists, and pharmacists.

The 1949 campaign, Whitaker and Baxter reported, resulted in the distribution of 55 million pieces of literature reaching approximately 100 million persons. Coupled with the attack on governmental programs was a successful effort to promote the sale of commercial health insurance policies under the slogan "The Voluntary Way is the American Way."[6] The techniques were new, skillful, and thorough. The major arguments in this and subsequent campaigns, however, were not new; they differed little from those that Morris Fishbein had used extensively and elaborated fully during the 1930s. Madison Avenue added the public relations techniques, but medicine itself had already refined the arguments.

The 1950 campaign made use of the same techniques that had proven so effective in 1949. In addition, physicians formed political committees in many congressional districts. In Wisconsin, for example, "Physicians for Freedom" helped defeat Democrat Andrew Biemiller in his bid for reelection to the U.S. House of Representatives. Tactics included posters, advertisements, and campaign literature included with monthly bills to patients. Biemiller was an outspoken advocate of health care legislation. Similarly, Senator Claude Pepper (D–Fla.) lost his Senate seat partly as a result of organized medicine's opposition. The actions of a Tallahassee hospital were representative of the campaign. Patients there found cards reading "This is the season for canning Pepper" on their food trays.[7]

In 1952 an organization calling itself the National Professional Committee for Eisenhower and Nixon mailed its political literature from the address of the former National Education Campaign. Although the AMA officially was neutral in the election, the National Professional Committee used letterheads listing former AMA president Elmer L. Henderson as chair and former presidents John Wesley Cline and Ernest F. Irons as vice-chairs—it also included the name of Whitaker and Baxter. A similar "Physicians for Stevenson" organization had no AMA officials as sponsors or any other evidence of AMA support.[8] With the election of a Republican administration avowedly hostile to governmental health insurance, which it agreed would have been "socialized medicine," the formal public relations or propaganda campaigns that the AMA financed lessened in intensity.

The AMA placed its members on the alert again, however, in 1957. Representative Aime Forand, a Rhode Island Democrat, introduced his first Forand Bill (H.R. 9467). Forand's bill would have paid for certain hospital and surgical services for patients who were receiving Social Security benefits. He re-introduced his bill in 1959 in the Eighty-sixth Congress (H.R. 4700). The Ways and Means Committee held hearings on Forand Bills in 1957, 1958, and 1959 but took no action. On 31 March 1960, the committee finally rejected the plan by a vote of 17 to 8—ironically, the same vote by which it was to accept the Medicare proposal five years later.

In the same year, Senator John F. Kennedy (D.–Mass.) introduced a bill similar to those that Forand had introduced. After his presidential nomination, Kennedy made his support of the measure a major campaign point. His bill failed in the Senate by a vote of 55 to 41, defeated by a coalition of Republicans and Southern Democrats. In 1961, the Ways and Means Committee again held hearings in the House, and again took no action.

AMA opposition to Medicare during the Kennedy Administration reached a peak in 1962 in response to the Anderson-King Bill, sponsored by Representative Cecil King (D.–Calif.) and Senator Clinton Anderson (D.–N.M.). This bill would have provided direct payment to hospitals for services rendered to Social Security beneficiaries aged sixty-five and over. Supporters finally succeeded in attaching a modified version of the Bill, the Anderson-Javits Amendment (co-sponsored by Republican Senator Jacob Javits), to a House-approved public welfare bill. Opponents defeated the attempt by tabling the amendment in July of 1962. This was the climax of the controversy over Medicare prior to its actual passage three years later by the Eighty-ninth Congress.

The battle had been intense and bitter. Each side took its case to the people by means of virtually every medium of mass communication—newspapers, magazines, radio, and television, and each side sent prominent spokespersons into debate. The AMA found its champion in the person of the chair of its speakers' bureau, Edward Annis, M.D. Almost singlehandedly Dr. Annis bore the burden of his association's speechmaking throughout the country. He debated frequently with such proponents of the legislation as union leader Walter Reuther and Senator Hubert Humphrey.

Annis also became editor-at-large of *Medical Economics*, a magazine devoted largely to the business side of medical practice, distributed free of charge to all physicians. In recognition of his service, the AMA elected Annis its president—the first in more than forty years who had not previously been a member of the House of Delegates, served on the Board of Trustees, or served on any of the councils and committees of the association.[9]

He proved to be a clever leader, and the AMA continued to make effective use of public relations experts. On 20 May 1962, President Kennedy appeared as speaker at a televised rally in Madison Square Garden on behalf of the Anderson-King Bill. His administration scheduled this as one of forty-two meetings across the country to generate support. The AMA thereupon dispatched half of its "task force on the Anderson-King Bill," headed by AMA's director of communication, Jim Reed, to New York to obtain paid radio-television time for a rebuttal and to handle relations with the press. The other half remained at AMA headquarters in Chicago to keep in touch with the association's executive director and its other key officials.[10]

The night following Kennedy's address, Annis spoke—also at Madison Square Garden, but this time before empty seats. Recognizing that the AMA could not hope to match the drawing power of the president or generate the same enthusiasm among a crowd, AMA strategists chose the empty seats deliberately to contrast with the wildly cheering audience that Kennedy had addressed, presenting themselves as the "little guys."[11] NBC stations throughout the country carried the Annis speech, except for the station in Boston. The Boston channel refused, saying that its policy was to refuse to sell time to organizations to present one side of controversial questions. The AMA immediately accused the station, which had carried Kennedy's speech, of "blacking out" one side of a controversy in the president's home town. Both sides thus had been accused of similar practices. The AMA long had the reputation of refusing to include in its own publications any opinion from a physician with whom the association disagreed.

Tom Hendricks, assistant to the AMA's executive director, was candid when interviewed about the extent of the publicity campaign against Medicare. He included as a part of that campaign a forthcoming *Reader's Digest* article by Representative Thomas B. Curtis (R.–Mo.), a member of the House Ways and Means Committee. Curtis strenuously opposed Medicare, but denied that he was speaking on behalf of any interest. Nevertheless, he coordinated his article in advance with AMA officials.[12]

Major organizations supporting Medicare were Aime Forand's national Council of Senior Citizens for Health Care through Social Security, the American Nurses Association, the National Association of Social Workers, the American Public Welfare Association, and a number of other social welfare and public health organizations.[13] The American Nurses Association (ANA) reported considerable pressure from physicians to change its stand and charged that many nurses had been forced to resign from the association by their physician employers. The ANA's Washington representative, Julia Thompson, testified during the Ways and Means Committee's hearings on the bill that medical societies in no less than thirty-five states had sought to pressure nurses' associations in those states to disavow the pro-Anderson-King stance of the national organization.[14]

Among the major organizations opposing the bill were the AMA, almost all insurance companies (with the notable exception of Nationwide Insurance Company, which endorsed the bill strongly), the National Association of Manufacturers, the United States Chamber of Commerce, the National Association of Retail Druggists, and most other professional dental and medical organizations. Although officially opposing the bill, the Blue Cross Association and the American Hospital Association were more willing than most opponents to compromise, and they worked rather closely with the administration in preliminary planning for the organization and administration of any proposal that might materialize. Both organizations spent many hours in meeting with federal representatives, who were also permitted to make numerous visits to hospitals and the administrative headquarters of several local Blue Cross plans.[15]

Much of the controversy revolved around charges that the Anderson-King Bill would create "socialized medicine." A typical example of an AMA leaflet that physicians distributed to their patients was one entitled "An Important Message from Your Doctor." It stressed compulsion and government control, and argued that the program would "place a third party—Washington bureaucrats—between the patient and the physician. It would place politics at the bedside of the ill," the leaflet said. Not only would the patient's "free choice of hospital and physician" be limited, but the proposed program "would eliminate the privacy of the patient-physician relationship, . . . making it possible for government clerks to examine the most intimate personal health records—records that are now a private matter between patient and physician."

Even in those days, the idea of confidentiality between physician and patient could hardly be taken seriously. There may not have been "government clerks" inserted into the relationship, but there certainly were hospital clerks, insurance-company clerks, physicians' aides, and others. Nevertheless, the leaflet was perhaps more moderate than many. Instead of charging that the Anderson-King Bill would provide socialized medicine, it said merely that it would be "the first step toward socialized medicine in this country, . . . a system that has resulted in the deterioration of medical care wherever it

has been tried." It described the need to work together to preserve America's high quality of medical care, and it concluded
with: "Let's keep politics out of medicine."

A leaflet entitled "It's *Your* Decision" assured readers that
organized medicine did favor "a *voluntary* program." It advocated "voluntary health insurance" and a program to help the
elderly poor who could not afford to purchase it. It warned
darkly of "socialized medicine" and said "we are not crying
'wolf' when we apply that term to the Anderson-King Bill,"
which, it said, "would mean socialized health care . . . immediately for all those over 65 eligible for Social Security and
eventually for every man, woman, and child in America." It
urged patients to write to Congress to oppose the bill.

In New Mexico, the Chaves County Medical Society placed
an advertisement in the *Roswell Daily Record* (27 May 1962),
endorsed by the District No. 5 Association of Registered
Nurses, the Chaves County Pharmaceutical Association, and
the Roswell Dental Society. It asked, "Can governments doctor? President Kennedy and his associates say YES. We, your
physicians, say NO. BUT, this is more than a medical issue. It
is an issue affecting not only the health of our people, but the
economic and political freedom of our country." The ad even
cited the statement in the Declaration of Independence that it
is the right and duty of the people to throw off a government
when that government "evinces a design to reduce them under absolute despotism." There was more than a hint here
that adoption of Medicare should cause the people to over-
throw the government!

The Roswell ad was somewhat more extreme than most, but
there were similar expressions published widely throughout
the United States. Some of the material was purely local, but
much was based on AMA-supplied models. All of the attacks
praised American health care as the best in the world, and
many of them contrasted it with the "failed socialized health
care" elsewhere. There were numerous declarations from local
associations and individual practitioners then and after Medi-

care's passage that they would refuse to treat Medicare patients. Some members even attempted to persuade the AMA to make such a refusal binding upon its membership. The attempts failed, but the AMA did seriously consider the idea.

One of the most interesting features of the campaign for and against the Anderson-King Bill was a recording, "Ronald Reagan Speaks Out Against Socialized Medicine." Reagan, then still an actor, prepared it for the AMA. The record was at the heart of the AMA's "Operation Coffeecup," a brilliant effort to encourage opponents of the Anderson-King Bill to write to senators and representatives urging that they vote against the proposal.

The letter accompanying the record was dated 15 April 1961. It was addressed to members of women's auxiliaries of the AMA, that is, to wives of physicians. There was an AMA auxiliary in every county in the country that had a county medical association.

The auxiliary members were instructed to invite friends and neighbors who agreed with them politically to listen to Reagan telling why the Anderson-King Bill would be socialized—and bad—medicine. They were to "put on the coffeepot," serve coffee, play the record, provide pen and paper for the guests to write their individual letters, collect and mail the letters (three from each person—one to her representative and one to each of her two senators), and report back to the AMA how many letters she had mailed. As interesting as the record's attack on Medicare was its perhaps less dramatic, but no less forceful, attack on Social Security itself. As Chapter 6 makes clear, Reagan's attitude toward Social Security was openly hostile until his successful presidential campaign of 1980. During that campaign he not only professed support for Social Security but specifically denied (in his debate with President Carter) that he had opposed the principles of Medicare.

The Operation Coffeecup campaign was to be kept as secret as possible. It resulted in an enormous flood of letters to Congress, and each letter was individually worded and individu-

ally handwritten. It was a brilliant tactic and contributed to
the defeat of the Anderson-King Bill and the Anderson-Javits
Amendment. It certainly helped hold off the adoption of
Medicare, and the secrecy also was largely effective. Although
there were some public reports of Operation Coffeecup, most
people were never aware of its existence, and members of
Congress tended to believe that the flood of letters following
the campaign was a spontaneous outpouring. Because of the
secrecy, few people today are aware of Reagan's role in delaying Medicare's adoption.

For many years, it appeared as though there were no copies
of the record still in existence. The AMA library reported that
it had lost its copy, and even the Reagan Collection in the
Hoover Institution at Stanford University failed to locate one.
The text of Reagan's speech finally was published, along with
some of the materials that accompanied the recording, but not
until 1989. Even then, the remarks that followed Reagan's on
the recording, comments by an unnamed announcer, remained missing.[16]

After nearly two decades of searching, a copy of the record
itself at last emerged.[17] The text of the record around which
the AMA built Operation Coffeecup appears in the Appendix.
It includes for the first time in print the summarizing comments that followed Reagan's remarks.

Reagan's speech indicates clearly that he was suspicious of
medical programs in general as tools of oppression. Their humanitarian aspects were "disguises." He did grudgingly ap-
prove a program to provide support "for people who need it,"
as did the AMA to head off a general program. The Kerr-Mills
scheme that he mentioned as a better alternative that already
existed ranged from poor to virtually worthless. In Kentucky,
for example, it provided as few as six days of hospitalization,
and those only for the destitute, and only for an acute and life-
endangering illness.

As for Social Security, Reagan conceded that there should
be "some form of saving" to provide for times of need. He

carefully avoided conceding that the government should be involved. In fact, his clear assumption was that Social Security was improperly supplanting "private saving, private insurance, pensions, programs of unions and industries." Rather than Social Security being bankrupt, as he charged in other talks, Reagan's words in his Operation Coffeecup presentation seemed to imply that it was *too* effective.

In September 1964 the Senate finally adopted an amendment to the Social Security Act similar to the Anderson-Javits Amendment. This was the first time that either house of Congress had managed to pass such legislation, but its destiny was death in conference committee. Discussion of this amendment had not been accompanied by the intensive public controversy that had surrounded the Anderson-King and Anderson-Javits proposals, probably because the opponents had become sure of themselves, even though Lyndon Johnson had assumed the presidency.

The only other favorable action on even a slightly related health care program before the Eighty-ninth Congress came in 1960, with adoption of the Kerr-Mills Act—the one that Reagan praised in "Operation Coffeecup." This actually was an amendment to the Social Security Act, becoming Title XVI, "Medical Aid to the Aged." Under Kerr-Mills, states received grants to assist in the health needs of the indigent and the "medically indigent" aged.

The AMA supported Kerr-Mills as a way of averting action upon the Forand Bill, or some other program of broader scope. AMA support did, however, indicate a small crack in the solid front by organized medicine against government involvement in health care or its economics. The crack ultimately widened to permit proposing the "Eldercare" program, which also called for federal support.

The AMA announced its proposal for Eldercare on 17 January 1962. It would have been a national insurance program for the aged under the auspices of Blue Shield plans. Blue Shield pays physicians' bills, not hospital costs. Shortly before the

AMA's announcement, the American Hospital Association and the Blue Cross Association on 3 January proposed a similar plan for hospital benefits, which the AMA rejected. Eldercare would have required the approval of each of the sixty-nine separate Blue Shield plans—it aroused little enthusiasm among them. The AMA said that Eldercare was its reaction to proposals to "socialize" medicine.

Abraham Ribicoff, Secretary of Health, Education, and Welfare, attacked the AMA's proposal vigorously. It would not have prevented physicians from charging patients over and above the amounts the plan would pay and had no provision whatever for the greatest charges: hospital costs. Organized medicine was not deterred, and as a last-ditch effort threw its resources into a massive publicity campaign, much of which was under the control of its political action committee, AMPAC (American Medical Political Action Committee).

AMPAC pursued its task with gusto. Its zeal was so great that when it was hardly a year old, it caused the AMA one of the greatest embarrassments in the history of the venerable organization and brought it face-to-face with a $400,000 suit for damages resulting from alleged fraud and libel. In November 1963, Paul Normile, director of the western Pennsylvania District 16 of the United Steelworkers of America, filed the suit against the AMA in the Washington, D.C., U.S. District Court.

The suit stemmed from a phonograph recording that the AMA produced in quantity and distributed by the thousands throughout the country. The recording purported to be of a speech by Normile at a political education meeting of a group of steelworkers in western Pennsylvania. The voice on the recording made rough threats in gangsterlike fashion as though extorting contributions from assembled union members to support the battle for Medicare by threatening those who did not "come across" with the "graveyard shift" and other unpleasantness. The voice was tough and the comments illiterate.

The President of the AFL-CIO, George Meany, asserted that the recording was an "absolute fraud." Normile denied that the voice was his or that he had made any such speech. Meany denied that there had been any such speech by anyone. The record jacket, entitled "The Voice of COPE" (the AFL-CIO's Committee on Political Education), contained a printed text of the recording and information to the effect that AM-PAC had obtained it from a union member, one "who opposes, as many members of the labor movement do, the high-pressure methods which C.O.P.E. resorts to in its efforts to dominate government at every level within the United States."

The jacket contained a message, signed by Donald E. Wood, M.D., chairman of the board of directors of AMPAC. Wood recommended that the record be played to make physicians aware that membership in AMPAC was essential for the maintenance of free medical practice. The AMA decided to withhold official comment on the suit until it became aware of the full details, but Dr. Annis called the charges "ridiculous" and merely an effort to divert attention from the issues.

The following January the judge rejected the union's plea that the AMA be ordered to apologize in the *Journal of the American Medical Association (JAMA)* for having distributed the record, ruling that it would be an admission of guilt. The court proceedings revealed that the record allegedly was purchased for twenty dollars on a dark street late at night from an unknown middleman. The AMA represented the suit as actually a dispute between organized medicine and organized labor regarding pending legislation. For a time, its spokesman maintained that it was merely an effort to discredit the association and said that they had not eliminated the possibility that the voice actually did belong to Normile—even though a speech expert that Normile had employed asserted that it was impossible. AMA executives admitted that they did not know whose voice was on the record, but they claimed that they had thought it to be authentic when they purchased it. They argued that they had a right to distribute it, because it dealt with pending legislation of great importance, and that the AMA therefore should not be held liable for damages. The judge refused to permit the record to be played in court, but he listened to a transcript that the attorney for Normile and the union read.

After a long delay and much bargaining and hesitation, the AMA announced on 11 March 1966 that it had arrived at a settlement out of court with Normile and issued a statement that was printed in the following issue of the *Journal of the American Medical Association (JAMA)* and also on page one of the *AFL-CIO News* for 12 March:

> In March 1963, the American Medical Association was sent a tape recording of what purported to be a political fund raising speech made in Pennsylvania by a Pittsburgh labor leader, Mr. Paul Normile, director of District 16, United Steelworkers of America. Believing in good faith that the tape recording was authentic, the AMA reproduced it and the American Medical Political Action Committee produced and distributed a booklet entitled "The Voice of COPE," containing the text of the speech and a phonograph record made from the tape as evidence of the tactics which they believed labor used in support of its objectives.
>
> Mr. Normile thereafter filed a lawsuit alleging that he never made the speech in question. Distribution of the tapes and records was immediately voluntarily discontinued pending full investigation of his contention. As a result of its exhaustive investigation, the AMA is now satisfied that Mr. Normile did not make the speech in question. In fairness to him, the statement that he did so is retracted. Furthermore, all copies of the tape recording and the AMPAC booklet and record in the possession of AMA or AMPAC have been destroyed. To prevent further playing of the recording, it is urged that any person having a copy of either the tape or the record take similar action. The AMA sincerely regrets the error.

The embarrassment that caused the professional association to wait for two and one-half years is understandable.

Moreover, the delay possibly permitted any effect the record was having to continue for a while. By the time of the apology, the issue was moot.

In 1965, the acknowledged legislative master Lyndon B. Johnson not only held the presidential office but had been elected in his own right—and with the largest percentage of the popular vote in American history. LBJ employed a burst of activity to make Medicare a top priority, and the program finally materialized. Ironically, despite the fierce opposition from organized medicine, the Medicare program catapulted American physicians into even greater affluence than previously. Their elderly patients—many of whom had previously been destitute and receiving charity care—became able to pay their bills.

The same amendments that added Medicare raised the Social Security tax rate to 4.2 percent as of 1966 and increased the taxable wage base to $6,600. It also brought self-employed M.D.s under coverage, adding them to D.O.s, the group of physicians already covered. M.D.s had fought strongly, and for a time successfully, to resist being included. This resistance to inclusion by one group but not the other demonstrated the purely political nature of the issue, inasmuch as their practices were and are identical.

Benefit increases came in 1968, 1971, and 1972, with the wage base increasing to $7,800 in 1968 and $9,000 in 1972. In 1973 the wage base went to $10,800 and the tax to 5.85 percent. Significantly, the 1972 amendments also added automatic cost-of-living adjustments to benefits, tying them to the Consumer Price Index. The adjustments were to begin in January of 1975.

For the first time, however, a cloud appeared on Social Security's horizon. The next chapter will examine the end of expansion, the beginning of retrenchment, and the explosion of politics—politics attacking the Social Security system itself.

Although Social Security and Medicare had emerged and expanded to meet an obvious need, the same ideology that had opposed social insurance in the beginning managed once more to come to the surface. That ideology held all government action promoting the general welfare to be suspect. Social Security's popularity with the people had been its shield against the selfish and the ideologues. It would need that shield as the battle intensified.

5

Frightening Facts? Or Persistent Politics?

The first period of retrenchment in Social Security's history came not long after the 1972 amendments. Fears of a cash flow shortage caused the Nixon administration to delay the automatic adjustments half a year, until June 1975. Despite this delay, the feared shortage did develop in 1977. It was no crisis, but it was clear that something needed to be done—and it was. Nevertheless, long exposure to rhetoric such as Reagan's had conditioned many members of the public to react with unjustified nervousness.

With the support of the Ford administration, Congress then raised the tax to 6.13 percent as of 1979 and put into effect the increased tax rates and wage base amounts that previously had been scheduled for later years. The 1977 changes also prevented the practice of "double-dipping" for civil servants who qualified for Social Security as a result of earlier employment; they could no longer receive full Civil Service retirement benefits and full Social Security benefits simultaneously.

During the 1980s, another cash-flow problem suggested that the 1977 changes had been insufficient to ensure fiscal soundness. Congress responded to the situation in 1983, radically revising the scheme that had evolved through the years, which had come to function largely in a pay-as-you-go manner. Discarding pay-as-you-go, Congress opted for full financing and provided for the accumulation of enormous trust funds in anticipation of the pressure that would develop some years later when the baby boom generation retired. It also for the first time subjected Social Security benefits to income tax. Those beneficiaries whose income exceeded a set amount were required to include 50 percent of their benefits as income when calculating their tax. In 1993, the amount rose to 85 percent; in other words, only 15 percent of their benefits remained tax free for the more affluent taxpayers.

The 1983 revisions also prevented states from changing their minds and opting out of the system once they had brought their employees under Social Security coverage. Finally, in the hope that it would remove any doubt about the ability of income to balance outgo permanently, Congress provided for a gradual increase in the age of full retirement from sixty-five to sixty-seven, delayed the impending cost-of-living adjustment, and accelerated the schedule of tax-rate increases. Under the 1983 law, the normal retirement age increases from sixty-five to sixty-six for workers who become sixty-two in the year 2005, and increases to sixty-seven for those who become sixty-two in 2022 or thereafter. As noted in Chapter 1, projections were that these changes would bring the system permanently into balance. Although there is no real reason to believe that those projections were not valid, everyone proclaims that Social Security is once again in trouble.

The major concern is fueled by demographics—or rather by an enormous and well-financed propaganda campaign to convince both policymakers and the public that demographics portend disaster. No informed observer who remains relatively free from ideological blinders can deny that Social Security has been an enormously successful government program. It has ensured the welfare of countless numbers of Americans. Many observers now believe, however, that population shifts, and increasing life expectancies have changed the situation and are creating clear dangers.

The argument goes as follows: As baby boomers retire, the number of people receiving retirement benefits escalates, while the number of workers paying into the system in relation to the number of retirees shrinks. Thus, progressively fewer workers will be supporting the system, which must make payments to progressively more beneficiaries. As a matter of fact, as I pointed out in Chapter 1, the actuaries anticipated this change and planned for it.

Much of the concern results from publicity given to the reports of the trustees of the trust funds. The trustees make annual reports on the state of the trust funds, including projections far into the future. As Chapter 1 points out, they do so because the law requires them to do so. They do concede, however, that the longer term the forecast, the less the validity. Projections for thirty years in the future would be at best highly unreliable. As mentioned before, projections could not anticipate the dissolution of the Soviet Union or the achievement of a balanced budget. In early 1999 the budget surplus was growing at a far greater rate than the best projections had indicated less than half a year previously.

Because of the unreliability of long-term projections, the trustees' reports received hardly any attention until the early 1990s. At that time they began to use a different set of assumptions in making their calculations. For some years after the 1983 amendments, their projections had consistently shown favorable fund balances far into the future. When their assumptions changed, however, so did their projections. Social Security's enemies seized on the new projections and began a publicity blitz that blanketed the news media with pessimistic and startling predictions of "bankruptcy." Most of the media treated their press releases as legitimate news items, inundating the public with scare propaganda regarding Social Security.

The trustees' intermediate (as opposed to high cost—more pessimistic—and low cost—more optimistic) projections for several years in the 1990s, up to and including those for 1997, predicted that the Old Age, Survivors, and Disability Insurance (OASDI) Trust Funds would receive sufficient income to cover all benefits until the year 2013. Then, the increasing benefit outgo would begin to exceed income and would cut into the accumulated assets, which at that time should be somewhere around $1.3 trillion. By 2029, the trust funds would be gone. Only the income would remain, and that would be able to pay only three-fourths of the current benefit level.

What was hidden beneath the propaganda was that the trustees also issued *optimistic* projections. Based on more optimistic assumptions, these projections removed the dangers to the far future or eliminated them entirely. (There were, of course, also pessimistic projections based upon the most unfavorable assumptions, but these are so unrealistic that—except for rare instances—even the critics have ignored them as too unbelievable to be effective in their propaganda. The intermediate projections are sufficiently pessimistic for their purposes, and using them in their calculations enables Social Security's enemies to claim that their approach is "reasonable.")

The optimistic projections received no publicity! They were based upon favorable performance of the economy. The public, misled by the drumbeat of opposition, failed to notice that the economy between 1993 and 1997—the years when the projections were remaining constant—was exceeding all expectations by far. If the trustees were aware of the increased performance, they refused to permit it to influence their "intermediate" projections.

The 1998 projections finally began to take note of America's powerful economy. The trustees' report for 1998 moved the dreaded "depletion year" from 2029 to 2032. In one year's time the great threat jumped three years into the future. The optimistic projections, of course, continued to anticipate no difficulty at any time in the future.

As Chapter 1 explains, there are many reasons to be skeptical of the pessimism of even the 1998 report. The trustees themselves caution against using their projections as though they are precise portrayals of what will happen. They also admit that all economic factors have been *more* favorable than projected after 1983, a time when the trustees' reports projected that the system would have a permanent surplus. It is significant that they admit that the 1990s projections of deficits result solely from their more pessimistic methods of calculation.

If there are good reasons to be skeptical of the trustees' pessimism, there are even more reasons to reject completely the arguments of those who would "reform" the system. In nearly all cases, their reforms are disguised steps toward killing Social Security.

Consider, for example, the critics' (not the trustees') use of demographics. At best, it is simpleminded; at worst, it is deceitful. There is no doubt that the population is aging. The number of elderly retirees will certainly increase in relation to the number of workers paying into the system. There is more to the story than this, however, although there are great efforts to prevent the public—and policymakers—from recognizing it.

First, the baby boomers will not draw upon the system forever. They will ultimately pass through the system like a bubble.

Second, the increasing life span is not what it has been portrayed as being. Much of it results from the declining rate of infant mortality. On average, the population lives much longer because fewer infants die, but the life expectancy of a sixty-five-year-old today is only a little longer than it was in 1940 when Social Security benefits began. According to a table available from the Social Security Administration web site, life expectancy at the age of sixty-five was 12.7 years in 1940 for a man and 14.7 years for a woman. In 1990, the figures were 15.3 and 19.6. The new retirement age of sixty-seven offsets two years of that gain, which leaves an average increase of less than two years.

Third, as the number of retirees increases, the number of those drawing benefits before retirement age—survivors and disability beneficiaries—will decline. This decline will serve as a partial offset to the increasing number of retirees.

Fourth, the relevant figure is not the number of elderly as compared to the young, but rather the number of beneficiaries compared to the number of people in the work force. "Today, 46 percent of Americans are in the labor force; when the boomers are all retired in about 2030, that number will decline slightly to 44 percent. In 1964, when the baby boomer population peaked, however, only 37 percent of Americans were in the labor force—a ratio considerably 'worse' than can be expected in the 21st century."[1] How can the work force be a greater proportion of the population than previously when there are additional numbers of elderly? The answer is simple. In 1964, it was rare for a woman to work. Because of the massive influx of women into the work force since then, it is common today for a woman to do so.

Also, immigrants, both legal and illegal, help the system. They pay into it and often retire back to their homelands and never draw benefits. Moreover, if the economy performs in the years to come with anywhere near the strength of the past few years, the robust economic activity would handle the baby boom retirements with little—or even more likely with no—strain. President Clinton's proposal to devote 62 percent of the budget surplus to the trust funds would make strain on those funds even less likely. Also, as he commented at the Kansas City forum on Social Security in April 1998, the budget is in balance, and projected surpluses for the next decade will be more than sufficient to pay off the bonds in the trust funds, or in other words, to pay back—without a tax increase—all the money the government has borrowed. This is a separate issue from the stability of the trust funds, and it is at least as important.

Those who advocate drastically changing Social Security are ignoring many important facts because of the fevered publicity. Perhaps the most important of all is the need to put things in perspective. What is the magnitude of the financial problem facing Social Security even if the pessimists are correct? Social Security is a large part of the national budget, of course, but it is a tiny part of the enormous American economy. Even if the shortfall projected by the trustees' most pessimistic assumptions were to materialize, the money required to make up the shortfall would be a smaller portion of the gross domestic product than increases in military expenditures during the Cold War years were. The economy clearly is powerful enough to absorb whatever it needs to, without major disruptions.

Despite the dire predictions, even the trustees' projections anticipate that a relatively small tax increase, only 2.19 percent of payroll (a tax on the worker of less than 1.1 percent), would ensure solvency at least through 2070. Moreover, as I have already indicated, the feared demographic shifts are considerably less fearful than the critics portray them. One such critic, Peter G. Peterson—who, along with former Senators Paul Tsongas and Warren Rudman, founded the Concord Coalition devoted to balancing the budget and reducing "entitlements"—brought together, in May 1996, the figures that bombard citizens throughout the media and political discussions. Focusing on his account should help clarify the real situation.

In a strongly worded article predicting catastrophe unless there are drastic changes to Social Security, Peterson wrote, "In 1960 there were 5.1 taxpaying workers to support each Social Security beneficiary. Today there are 3.3. By 2040 there will be no more than 2.0—and perhaps as few as 1.6."[2] Robert Eisner, a former president of the American Economic Association and professor emeritus of economics at Northwestern University, responded to Peterson's article by demonstrating that these dreaded figures overlook some important factors.

"We are told," he wrote, "that there are now almost five people of working age—20 to 64—for every potential depen-

dent aged 65 or over, and by 2030 that ratio will fall to less
than 3 to 1." What these figures overlook, he noted, is that
"the relevant numbers . . . relate to all potential dependents,
those below as well as above working age. Currently, for every
1,000 people of working age there are 709 young and old potential dependents. The intermediate projection puts the
number in 2030 at 788. That means that each 1,000 people of
working age would have to support 1,788 people—themselves
and their dependents—instead of 1,709, only a 4.62% increase
in their burden."[3] This is hardly the catastrophe that the critics predict.

It is unwise—and certainly "unconservative"—to make radical shifts in policy based on projections over decades. Long-
term economic forecasting is about as reliable as long-term
weather forecasting. The strength of the economy since 1993
has been far better than economists predicted—even while its
strength was increasing. Given that strength, the trustee's optimistic forecasts are more likely to be correct than the "intermediate" (and pessimistic) ones—and, as I have demonstrated, even their pessimistic projections do not indicate
catastrophe.

Nevertheless, the intermediate forecasts make the headlines, and much of the media treatment is lurid. "Social Security is going bankrupt—again," began a *New York Times* article on the system's troubles. "In 1983, the Social Security
cupboard was nearly bare. This time around, the economic
and political crisis is coming in slow motion: the system's income from payroll taxes is expected to exceed pension outlays
until 2013." Then the "relentless growth of pensioners will
eat into Social Security's accumulated claims against the
Treasury, forcing Washington to raise taxes or slash spending
on other programs. And, for the first time in the 60-year history of Social Security, some of its friends are asking for fundamental change before the system cracks."[4]

The latter point is truly cause for concern. The persistent
drumbeat of criticism has indeed caused many strong support-

ers of Social Security to assume that basic changes are necessary. Social Security's critics, of course, go far beyond the supporters in suggesting change—and the changes they suggest would destroy the system.

Peter G. Peterson takes a destructive approach, which reveals a thinly veiled hostility to the very idea of social insurance. He would phase in his suggestions, but even introduced gradually, they would eliminate Social Security as it currently exists. Some of his recommendations are merely extensions of current policy, such as increasing the retirement age still further, to seventy. The more extreme provisions of his program call for government-mandated individual investment accounts to "supplement Social Security" initially, but over time they "might increasingly substitute for it."

He says that "all workers (in some combination with employers) should be required to contribute four to six percent of their pay—which, added to FICA, would come to a total contribution of 16–18 percent of pay." Why not simply increase taxes? Peterson's scheme ultimately would eliminate spousal and survivors' benefits, as is common—although unstated—with "privatization" proposals. They similarly would work toward the elimination of disability protection and Medicare as well.

The rationale for private investment is that historically the stock market has appreciated more than the interest paid on Social Security's investments in government securities. If this supposed advantage is indeed a problem, the solution to it is clear: simply increase the interest on the government securities so that Social Security's investments equal those of the stock market. However careful private investments may be, the potential for loss is always present. Aggregate increases in the stock market do not guarantee that individual investments are free from risk. President Clinton's plan to add to the trust funds from budget surpluses is another way to make the trust funds grow faster, a way that carries with it none of the risk of private investment.

Private accounts would appear to be more virtuous in Peterson's mind because they would make "tomorrow's retirees more self-sufficient." Just how this would be so he does not explain. The program would be mandated, not voluntary, and the retiree would not have the option of withdrawing funds in a lump sum upon retirement. The only difference would be that the return would not be fixed. Wise (or lucky) investing could bring a high rate of return; unwise (or unlucky) investing would bring poverty. In addition to this, he says that all federal benefits should be means tested (or "affluence tested," as he puts it).

Peterson noted that "some have said that an affluence test would constitute a tax on savings, and thus would discourage thrift," but that "there is no evidence to support this hypothesis." (!) It hardly seems hypothetical that a worker would see saving as counterproductive, if saving—thereby postponing consumption until retirement—would eliminate benefits that otherwise would be paid.

Worse, he recognizes that "it has also been said that an affluence test would undermine public support for Social Security and other universal social-insurance programs. The theory seems to be that we must bribe the affluent in order to ensure political support for benefits for the needy. This is dead wrong." To justify his opinion, he points to a Concord Coalition poll that reflected public support for "reductions in Social Security benefits to higher-income households."[5] The wording of the question here would make a dramatic difference, and he did not provide the wording. His use of "bribe the affluent" no doubt is indicative.

Regardless of how the question is worded, though, it is irrelevant to the basic issue, which is public support for the Social Security system. A universal system receives support because people perceive benefits as their right. Increasing numbers would refuse to subject themselves to the humiliation of proving their poverty to welfare workers if it were necessary in order to obtain benefits. If the public began to see benefits as denied them because of their affluence, public support clearly would dwindle. An obvious example here is the reduced level of support for public schools when large numbers of a jurisdiction opt out of the system and either have no children or send their children to private schools.

Despite the seriously negative implications of Peterson's suggestions, there are even more overtly hostile opponents of Social Security. Some purely ideological opponents simply resist the idea of government involvement in Social Security. *Washington Post* writer James K. Glassman is an example. "Polls show Americans know benefits have to be cut," he has written. "The system must be abandoned."[6] We can find similar sentiments on all sides.

A letter to the editor of *USA Today* is a case in point. The author, who identified himself as a professor of economics at Auburn University, wrote that "the answer clearly does not rest with politicians, more government management or higher taxes. Privatizing Social Security is the logical solution." (How this could be done without action by politicians he did not explain.) He suggested that the plan advocated by Harry Browne, the former Libertarian candidate for president, be the model. Simply "sell the federal lands and capital assets, including dams, pipelines, airports, unnecessary military bases and office buildings to American entrepreneurs. It would be more efficient," he said, "to put these assets in the private sector." His apparent justification? "I have always favored the notion of having a pension rather than being on Social Security."[7] So much for logic.

Economist Robert Eisner is one of the few participants to the controversy surrounding Social Security who has seen through the verbiage and concentrated on realities. In 1996 he wrote that we hear that we must "do something now" and that "most frequently that something turns out to be an open or disguised cut in benefits to the elderly. Other, less painful solutions entail some form of privatization to enable retirees to realize the higher returns associated with stock market investments. The facts are that there is no crisis in Social Security now and there is none looming in the future."

In fact, he noted that a mere 1 percent increase per year in productivity per worker, which as he points out is "well within experience," would "easily accommodate the increased number of people the working population will have to support. Indeed, it would be sufficient for a one-third increase in output and income per capita, ample to improve vastly the lot of all—the elderly, the young and those in their working primes." Over the last twenty years, productivity growth has exceeded what Eisner has calculated to be necessary.

Privatization may or may not have merits, he said, but it is in any event unnecessary. Even under the intermediate projections of the trustees, as I have noted above, whatever problem exists is minor, and more optimistic projections are more likely to be the accurate ones.[8] Yet no less important a figure than Federal Reserve Board Chair Alan Greenspan made headlines in January 1999 by announcing that for Social Security to survive, it would soon require either tax increases or benefit cuts.

Such pronouncements have so severely shaken public confidence that, as I said in Chapter 1, restoring full confidence will probably require more than mere reassurances. Unlikely as the intermediate projections are, it would be wise to take steps to ensure that the trust funds will stay strong no matter what the economy does. Eisner has in fact made some suggestions, and in this next section I will consider his proposals along with other possibilities.

Incremental Changes That Would Not Hurt, and Could Help, Social Security

Suggestions for incremental changes to Social Security generally take the form of gradual tax increases, benefit reductions, or a combination of the two. Benefit reductions should be ruled out. Too many beneficiaries rely on Social Security as their sole source of income, and—especially for those who must do so—benefits already are too modest. Raising the retirement age to seventy is nothing other than a benefit reduction, and that also should be ruled out.

Devoting a portion of the current Social Security program to private investments would also be a benefit reduction—it would reduce the amount available to pay Social Security benefits. The idea would result in varied rates of return, with some winners and inevitably some losers. It would be destructive to the principle of social insurance, and it should be rejected.

On the other hand, a voluntary program that would be an add-on to the current system would provide greater savings and benefit to the country. Only those who are relatively well off could benefit—others would have too little excess income to participate—but it might induce some citizens to participate who otherwise might not invest on their own. Robert Eisner has provided the details and benefits of such a program,[9] and President Clinton in his 1999 State of the Union address suggested another, his "USA accounts."

Tax increases in the current political climate are not likely to be acceptable and in any case are unlikely to be required. Nevertheless, despite the unreliability of the trustees' pessimistic projections, it would be wise for many reasons to reconsider the cap on the amount of income subject to FICA taxes. President Clinton, in his address to the Kansas City Forum on Social Security in April 1998, indicated a willingness to consider raising the cap beyond its normal increases based on the Consumer Price Index. He said, though, that he was opposed to eliminating it completely.

Objections to eliminating the cap can come from each of two opposite directions. If benefits continue to increase with average income, some would argue that benefits for the wealthy would be too high to be just; if benefits remained capped at the current level, some would argue (as the president did) that the wealthy would be paying too much for the return that they receive. But there are sound reasons for removing the cap entirely.

There is, of course, a precedent. Medicare taxes now have no cap. The wealthy pay more than others for the same benefits. There is also the fact that the current OASDI cap results in a regressive tax. (The wealthy at least pay a flat tax for Medicare.) True, the very poor are assisted by the earned income tax credit, but with a cap, the worker whose income exceeds the maximum is taxed at a progressively lower rate as income rises. It may be too strong to argue, as some critics have done, that the system requires the poor to pay for helping the poor, but there is enough truth to it to make anyone who is concerned about social justice somewhat nervous.

OASDI benefits are calculated to provide greater return for workers of low income than for those at higher levels. The benefit formula should continue to provide this income redistribution as the cap is raised, then ultimately removed; each increment above the current maximum should provide a decreasing return, until at a certain level, the return would be zero. At that level, the FICA tax should no longer be labeled "FICA" on the employee's withholding statement or tax return, but should become an income tax surcharge—still to be credited to the trust funds.

Other ways exist for shoring up the trust funds that would involve no additional taxation and would not affect the balance of the national budget. Opponents of Social Security frequently charge that FICA taxes would receive a higher rate of return if they were invested in the stock market. Although they frequently present misleading and deliberately confusing arguments that understate the earnings of the trust funds, and although they exaggerate the safety and return from the market, they have convinced some people that the trust funds earn too little.

Robert Eisner has come up with an ingenious solution: simply increase the rate of interest that the government pays on the bonds that the trust funds buy. Eisner also suggests earmarking a portion of the income tax to the trust funds. Currently, Americans pay FICA taxes but cannot deduct those taxes from income when calculating their income taxes. Eisner argues that the portion of the tax that results from "tax on tax" should be credited to the trust funds.

These two measures, he argues, would make up for the shortfall in the trustees' intermediate projections—assuming that a shortfall actually were to materialize. As he points out, in both cases "this would be merely a matter of bookkeeping, not affecting the debt held by the public, or the deficit, or the benefits paid out by Social Security. It would only change what the accountants are crediting to the funds and hence their balances," yet it could do much to restore public confidence.

President Clinton's proposal in the 1999 State of the Union address would be similar to the Eisner plan and would credit roughly two-thirds of any budget surpluses to the trust funds. This is an excellent proposal, and it would help prevent across-the-board tax cuts, which would be undesirable for many reasons. As for the president's additional proposal to invest a portion of this trust fund supplement in the stock market, as I pointed out above and in Chapter 1, it presents some dangers, including introducing risk. In any case, it is unnecessary.

Considering Eisner's arguments and the others I have given in this and previous chapters, it seems clear that Social Security is not facing a crisis, and that if it does have troubles, they are minor and can easily be fixed. Yet even mainstream journalistic sources—those that the right has convinced itself are "liberal"—have accepted the crisis mentality. Witness the *New York Times* article quoted above that claimed that "Social Security is going bankrupt—again." It provided the details of three varied approaches of those who call for revising Social Security. Former Social Security Commissioner Robert M. Ball's suggestion is called "patching" the current system. The other alternatives are described as "partial privatization" and "full privatization,"[10] with no mention that they would at best undermine, and at worst destroy, Social Security.

The article also did not bring out the extraordinary extent to which each of these plans resulted from an atmosphere that has been clouded—if not poisoned—by a consistent, coherent, and coordinated attack upon the whole notion of social insurance. Yet only a full understanding of that attack can provide an answer to the question of how, if any problems are in fact minor, the campaign against Social Security has managed to convince much of the public that a crisis exists. I have already given some account of this attack and the history behind it. It is now time to look at it in detail.

6

The Enemies Regroup

Rallying 'Round Reagan

The intense and open opposition that burst into flame after Social Security's passage was especially fierce during the presidential election of 1936, but it did not last long. Public support for the system was so obviously strong that politicians immediately halted their criticism. Attacking Social Security became politically perilous. From then until the 1970s there were few overt attacks. Of the few that did materialize, most came from elements recognized as being right-wing extremists. They tended not to be taken seriously.

One exception came from the ranks of professionals and generally was not well publicized. The American Medical Association, of course, was primarily concerned with preventing any government program that provided health care, but it appeared to have a broader concern as well. There was at least some evidence of hostility toward the entire Social Security system. Perhaps it resulted from the theoretical relationship of government health care to social insurance in general and to Social Security in particular.

As mentioned in Chapter 4, in 1920 the American Medical Association had adopted a resolution expressing its opposition to any government involvement in providing health care or paying health expenses. Morris Fishbein affirmed in the AMA's 1947 official history that the policy had not changed. It was recognition of that policy—and fear of organized medicine's political power—that led FDR in 1935 to omit health care from the original Social Security Act. He believed, with considerable justification, that to include health coverage might have energized the AMA to direct its wrath against the entire social insurance program.

Despite FDR's caution, the AMA's opposition did come to expand beyond health issues to include Social Security itself. The December 1939 issue of the *Journal of the American Medical Association* included an editorial saying:

> Indeed, all forms of security, compulsory security, even against old age and unemployment, represent a beginning invasion by the state into the personal life of the individual, represent a taking away of individual responsibility, a weakening of national caliber, a definite step toward either communism or totalitarianism.

This statement alone would not be sufficient evidence: The association's position is that official policy statements come only from resolutions by its House of Delegates, not from statements by its president or editorials in its official journal. And in fact it is true that the AMA avoided taking a position pro or con on passage of the Social Security Act when it testified before Congress in 1935 during the bill's consideration.

Nevertheless, in 1949 the AMA's House of Delegates itself did make the official position on Social Security rather plain. That year it adopted a formal resolution declaring that "So-called 'Social Security' is in fact a compulsory socialistic tax which has not provided satisfactory insurance protection for individuals where it has been tried but, instead, has served as the entering wedge for establishment of a socialistic form of government control over the lives and fortunes of the people."[1] Despite this resolution, the AMA has consistently tried to defend itself against charges that it opposed Social Security merely by repeating that it did not take a position on Social Security legislation.

Because of Social Security's popularity, overt opposition such as that from the AMA rarely entered into the discourse of formal politics. But there was a small cloud on the horizon that over the years grew into a hurricane of hostility to the social insurance program that had become as American as apple pie. As early as 1954 one spokesman began to gain prominence. There gradually coalesced around him those elements that had long opposed Social Security but had been relatively quiet since the days of the New Deal. That spokesman was actor Ronald Reagan, who hosted *G.E. Theater* on television.

Ronald Reagan and "The Speech"

As part of General Electric's public relations program, Reagan developed what he came to call simply "The Speech," which he gave at hundreds of meetings around the country. It was in fact an adaptation of The Speech that Reagan used on behalf of the AMA's "Operation Coffeecup" in 1962, altering it to make it primarily an attack on the idea of Medicare, with only a glancing blow at Social Security.

Kurt Ritter, a scholar who studies communication, produced a careful study of The Speech in 1968[2]. He found that it varied somewhat according to the audience, but the variations were confined essentially to emphases and order of topics. The Speech always included such themes as the evils of "big government," the dangers of communism, the threat from centralization, and the insufferable burden of high taxes. Reagan warned emotionally of the peril from governmental paternalism, and pointed to the "failure" of Social Security.

Such overt attacks on Social Security had become rare since the early days when critics discovered how popular the program was with the public. Officeholders were especially careful in most instances to give the impression that they were strong supporters. Republicans as well as Democrats had endorsed Social Security through the years. Both parties had presided over expanded coverage and benefit increases.

Reagan, though, was a private figure. Since he did not hold public office, he was under few if any constraints that would cause him to hide his views.

By the early 1960s, he had spoken countless times around the country in virtually every section. The more he spoke, the more strongly he stressed his opposition to Social Security. He began to give that opposition a headline role in his presentations. For example, he gave The Speech to the Phoenix Chamber of Commerce on 30 March 1961 and again that year on 28 July to the Orange County Press Club in California.[3] At both presentations, Reagan said that proposals for health care were traditionally "one of the easiest first steps to impose statism on a people," because such proposals could be "disguised" as humanitarianism. In each speech, he went on to say that the Social Security system was an intrusion on liberty. Moreover, he thundered, it was bankrupt.

Now, remember that Reagan was speaking in 1961! Think of all the checks that the system has faithfully, and without fail, mailed in the many decades since those and his other speeches. Those who wish to see for themselves what he actually said can find many of these addresses printed in his collected papers, or in the relevant volumes of *Vital Speeches*, or simply turn to the Appendix in this book to read his Operation Coffeecup speech, "Ronald Reagan Speaks Out Against Socialized Medicine."

Reagan's skillful presentation of The Speech brought him to the attention of some of the more conservative Republican Party officials. He impressed them, despite the unanimous opinion of his critics that he was simplistic and a political extremist. Seeking to harness his admirable and unquestioned powers of persuasion, these conservatives invited Reagan in 1964 to present a thirty-minute nationwide television broadcast defending Senator Barry Goldwater's doomed presidential candidacy.

He did so, presenting The Speech in Senator Goldwater's behalf on 27 October. It was electrifying. Although Goldwater lost, Reagan won. His forceful talk began the political journey that carried him not only to two terms as governor of California, but ultimately to election and re-election as president of the United States.

However scornful Reagan was of Social Security in his years as spokesman for G.E., and however much that scorn had increased by the time of the Kennedy administration, his opinion continued to become even harder as time passed. In giving The Speech to the National Association of Manufacturers on 8 December 1972, he told his audience to consider Social Security. "I have to say," he said to the group, "that if you couldn't come up with a better idea than that, you wouldn't still be in business."[4]

Although he became skillful at shifting emphases in The Speech according to his audience, Reagan consistently adhered to his fundamental beliefs from his days as a corporate spokesman until his assumption of high political office. He was too skilled as a politician, though, not to be aware that it was important for him to project a nonthreatening image to the general public. The more hard-edged attacks he reserved for talks to private groups or for otherwise less well publicized addresses. When speaking to general audiences, he was careful to stress, as Ritter put it so well, his "eagerness to solve the problems of age, health, poverty, and housing 'without compulsion and without fiscal irresponsibility.'"

On television he attempted to portray himself as reasonable, if nothing else. His radio addresses, however, were another matter. They tended to reach only the true believers and received little if any general publicity. In speaking to the more restricted body of listeners, he discarded many of his television-induced inhibitions.

There is no easily available source for the contents of his radio addresses, and their texts are very difficult to find. Some of them are available in the Reagan Collection at the Hoover Institution at Stanford University. Also, early in Reagan's presidency the journalist Ronnie Dugger managed to locate several more, which he published in 1983 in his excellent and quite critical study, *On Reagan: The Man and His Presidency.*

It is instructive to examine what Reagan said in his less guarded moments. In 1975 he emphasized Social Security in his radio broadcasts and devoted three programs specifically to the subject. The Hoover Institution has written transcripts of the texts, but they are undated except for the penciled notation "(1975)." Dugger identified the dates as September 24, 25, and 29. In the first program, Reagan said flatly that "social security reduces your chances of ever being able to enjoy a comfortable retirement income." He described Social Security as "a sure loser" in the second program, and supplemented that judgment with what seemed to be absolute statistical precision. His numbers, however, had no relation whatever to reality—giving meaningless numbers was a practice for which Reagan became notorious. "If there were no Social Security," he said, "wages would be 15% higher and interest rates 28% lower." Social Security taxes should be eliminated, he said in the third program, with the employer's share of the tax added to workers' salaries. Workers then could choose to invest in a private pension plan that the government would insure or could choose to invest in the option of a series of "new U.S. Retirement Bonds with annuity pay off."[5] This was an early shot, however feeble it may have seemed at the time, in a battle that since has escalated into a full-scale war designed to "privatize"—a euphemism for "eliminate"—Social Security.

Note that Reagan's early proposals contained the basic elements still present in so many efforts that purport to "reform" the massive system. Such efforts clearly are thinly disguised attempts to eliminate or at least to narrow social insurance. They tend to describe Social Security as if it were nothing but a pension program and allege that workers would benefit if they replaced Social Security with private investment. That is dubious, and it certainly would not be social insurance. It would also fail to provide for the full population, and that failure would increase the social ills of the country.

If Reagan recognized this problem, he disregarded it—as have the other critics who have followed his lead. Moreover, even if it were correct that private investment always brings higher returns and even if employers were to continue to provide their share of what currently is the Social Security tax so that workers could invest it, workers would lose Medicare, disability protection, and survivors' protection, as well as inflation protection for their benefits.

As mentioned earlier, the Social Security Administration's Office of the Actuary estimates that to replace Social Security's disability coverage on the private market would require a $207,000 policy. Private survivors' protection equaling that of Social Security would require a policy worth $307,000. Even disregarding the loss of Medicare and inflation protection for retirement benefits, that would be an enormous price to pay to satisfy the ideological prejudices of those who are firmly convinced that government cannot function well—even when they can see that by objective measures it is doing so.

The ideological approach of Social Security's enemies who follow in Reagan's footsteps is anything but conservative. The essence of conservatism is caution regarding change and suggestions for social engineering. The calls for drastic changes to Social Security come from the group in America that portrays itself as most conservative, yet those calls are explicitly radical and would have major and far-reaching consequences.

The modern enemies of Social Security were fortunate that their first and most influential spokesman had a genius for disguising the extremism of his views. On 28 October during the 1980 presidential campaign, former Governor Reagan was approaching the pinnacle of his career. He faced President Carter on television.

The president was well prepared and had his facts in order. He charged that Reagan had begun his political career campaigning against Medicare. Reagan, in rejoinder, charmed the audience, received friendly laughter, and seized control of the confrontation when he said, "There you go again." His opposition to Medicare, he said, was merely because he favored a better program, not that he opposed "the principle of providing care" for senior citizens. There is no evidence that President Carter harbors any bitterness about the exchange, but it would be understandable if he did.

Carter had been referring to the recording discussed in detail in Chapter 4, "Ronald Reagan Speaks Out Against Socialized Medicine." As the record's text indicates, there can be absolutely no question that Reagan in 1961 had served as the heart of the AMA's Operation Coffeecup and that the purpose of Operation Coffeecup was to combat not only the Medicare proposal but "the principle of providing care" by government action. Even if we ignore his other speeches, Reagan's words on the AMA's recording establish beyond any doubt the truth of Carter's charge that Reagan opposed—and opposed most strenuously—any form of social insurance, or any governmental involvement in providing health coverage to American citizens. Reagan triumphed that year, in part, by denying his clearly documented and often expressed hostility to Social Security and Medicare.

The 1980 election not only defeated Jimmy Carter, but for the first time since the beginning of Social Security it brought to the presidency a long and determined foe of social insurance. Ronald Reagan in the campaign had professed to support the system and had promised to preserve and protect it. A few months after he took office, however, his administration proposed sweeping reductions in benefits for future beneficiaries, elimination of the minimum benefit (even for those already receiving it), and other restrictions. There was a huge public outcry that caused his administration to retreat from most of its proposals and caused the president to promise never again to touch Social Security.

Nevertheless, some benefits—such as those to college students, if they were children of deceased workers, and the minimum benefit—were eliminated. Congress did restore the minimum benefit to those who had already been receiving it, but only to them. The administration was forced to apologize, saying that when it struck those beneficiaries from the benefit rolls, it had not intended to harm them!

Shortly after the beginning of the first Reagan term in the White House, Ronnie Dugger called him a "dedicated foe of Social Security." Reagan, he wrote, "regards it as welfare, which he detests." He noted that Reagan agreed in 1964 with Goldwater that Social Security should be made voluntary, in 1975 had "in effect proposed to abolish the whole system," and in 1978 had declared the system to be in effect bankrupt. "From the White House he has led a war on the Social Security system," Dugger wrote.[6] The bankruptcy charge, as we have seen, was not a new theme; Reagan had made the same charge since the 1950s.

Laurence Barrett, another journalist who examined the Reagan administration in the early 1980s, provided evidence that gives credence to Dugger's charge that Reagan attacked Social Security from within the Oval Office. Barrett documented that presidential aides knew that the massive Social Security cuts included in administration proposals in 1981 were more than double any that could have been needed to ensure the system's solvency. In addition, the proposals called for massive reductions in benefits.[7] Although, as mentioned above, public reaction to such excesses did force the administration to halt its overt attacks on Social Security and to restore the minimum benefit to those who previously were receiving it, that benefit vanished for future beneficiaries; since that time, retirees of extremely low earnings have no guaranteed minimum payment. President Reagan's rush to soothe the public and to promise that there would be no more cuts to Social Security was a political necessity, but it must have been as painful to him as loss of the minimum benefit had been to a poverty-stricken retiree.

If any questions remain about the administration's intentions—or about Reagan's preferences—Reagan's own budget director, David Stockman, set them to rest. As the designer of

"Reaganomics," Stockman was the author of much of the Reagan economic policy. He admitted that the phrase "future savings to be identified,"—the phrase that he used to "explain" the more than $40 billion in unspecified cuts in the initial budget that Reagan proposed to Congress—was nothing other than "a euphemism for 'We're going to go after Social Security.'"[8] Barrett said that when Reagan took office, he could not resist taking "one more whack at the Social Security system," even though it was clear that he would have to pay a political price to do so.[9]

Reagan's Legacy: The War Against Social Security

Reagan had a genius for appealing to the people and for portraying himself as "reasonable." When he secured the Republican presidential nomination, the public appeared quickly to forget that almost immediately before he became a candidate of a major party and within a year of his becoming president, Reagan had represented the far-right fringe of American politics. As president he had to abandon some of his right-wing goals. He failed to achieve his long-term goal of eliminating Social Security. In fact, he had to shift tactics to abandon direct attacks and advocate more subtle restrictions.

By this shift of tactics, however, Reagan did achieve some of his goals, including some benefit reductions. He also managed to manipulate the system to reduce progressivity in income taxes and to secure a drastically lower level of income taxation for upper-income taxpayers. As Republican political analyst Kevin Phillips reported, Social Security taxes rose to 36 percent of federal tax receipts from 31 percent, and the share of income taxes dropped from 47 percent to 45 percent.[10]

There were other consequences of Reagan's efforts as well, and it is these that we see in today's discussions of Social Security. Reagan's rhetoric and that of his followers had an effect. Those who had always opposed the principle of social insurance with its government involvement had begun for the first time to have some success in influencing others with their arguments—sometimes even others who were supporters of Social Security. Many of the arguments were misleading at best, and were deliberately so. What is clear to those who look is that even so they have had some effect.

Reflecting the influence of Reagan's success, the mainstream of American politics moved sharply to the right. Encouraging this shift with regard to Social Security was the skillful, and constant, use of misleading political rhetoric designed to generate conflict among different age groups, squeezing Social Security in the middle. In 1984, a Republican senator from Minnesota, David Durenberger, founded "Americans for Generational Equity" (AGE), designed to create questions about the "prudence, sustainability, and fairness of federal old age benefit programs."[11]

Within a few years, Durenberger's financial irregularities brought him into disrepute, and AGE disbanded. Before vanishing, however, it accomplished substantial mischief. Regardless of the elusive nature of the notion of "generational equity" (or inequity), AGE's activities created the perception that it was meaningful. As the thoughtful scholar Jill Quadagno has pointed out, all future policy choices will have to "take generational equity into account."[12] The disappearance of such an influential group leaves a vacuum which cannot exist for long.

Into that vacuum stepped Peter Peterson, a former secretary of commerce and an anti–Social Security zealot. He hit the equity issue hard and even made the preposterous charge that Social Security was "a direct cause of our federal deficit."[13] Helping to found the Concord Coalition, Peterson created an organization that, even though it contains many well-meaning members, has nevertheless been his tool in his strenuous efforts to undermine Social Security.

Some of the most perceptive analysts of social policy in the United States have made explicit the true nature of the Concord Coalition:

> Nominally dedicated to the purpose of educating Americans about the hard financial choices the nation will be confronting, the coalition reiterates the conservative position that government spending favors older, more affluent Americans at the expense of a younger generation that is already under financial distress. In addition to encouraging younger Americans to see themselves as needy and to see the elderly as an affluent group not deserving of public support, the coalition is not . . . [above] the use of scare tactics. It has warned, for example, that the failure to transform Social Security may bring on a generational war. And given their own residualist political agenda, Peterson and other coalition members have been ready to lead it.[14]

Peterson and his coalition members are not alone. Two clearly defined groups are at the heart of the effort to eliminate Social Security. The Cato Institute, a libertarian think tank and activist group, joins with Third Millennium, Citizens for a Sound Economy, and others to provide ideological fervor from a dedicated cadre of activists who simply do not believe that government should be involved in social welfare or large-scale social policies. Funding comes from Wall Street. Brokerage houses and investment firms would stand to reap untold billions in fees and commissions if even a small portion of Social Security were to become private. Some time ago, Trudy Lieberman exposed the nature of the financial power arrayed against Social Security. Her revealing article in *The Nation* received too little attention.[15]

As Lieberman reported, Leila Bate of Citizens for a Sound Economy is candid about the group's aims. It plans to spend "millions" in order to encourage privatization. When CSE "educated" congressional interns at a "Youth Summit" on Social Security in 1996, the interns left the sessions, Bate reported, with a "sense of the need to reform the system." She has remarked that it is important to have the "average American" accept the idea that Social Security must be radically revised if the group is to be successful.[16]

Echoing her comments is Jeanette Nordstrom of the National Center for Policy Analysis, another group that has attacked Social Security since the late 1980s. It spends hundreds of thousands of dollars on seminars, forums, and various media activities that she describes as parts of a "product line." The approach? Purely that of a sales pitch—appeal on the one hand to greed, on the other to fear—fear that Social Security faces a crisis "and needs a radical makeover." She has remarked that "the same clear, concise message must come from every direction," and one of the aims of that message is "to break the strong tie between the taxes employees pay during their working years and their right to a pension later on."[17]

Third Millennium is a small organization purporting to speak for the young. It has only a handful of employees, but they flood the media with monographs and op-ed pieces. One of its largest contributors is—surprise—Peter Peterson. It was from this group that the media were bombarded with the "finding" from a poll designed for it by the Republican pollster Frank Luntz and by Mark Siegel that young people were more likely to believe in UFOs than they were to believe that they would ever collect Social Security. The well-publicized finding, however, was a fraud, as Lawrence Jacobs and Robert Shapiro, two scholars of public opinion, have demonstrated:[18]

The Third Millennium's UFO survey has become the flagship for the presumption that confidence in Social Security has collapsed. The UFO survey, however, has been falsely sold. Journalists conveyed the impression that respondents had weighed the relative likelihood of UFOs existing and Social Security surviving and concluded that UFOs were more probable. In fact, the survey never offered respondents a direct comparison; instead, it offered two separate questions, with the Social Security question appearing fifth and the UFO question fourteenth (as the survey's last substantive question before some standard demographic items).

A 1997 survey by the Employee Benefit Research Institute (EBRI) offered respondents the direct choice that Third Millennium falsely claimed to have posed. EBRI asked, "Which do you have greater confidence in: receiving Social Security benefits after retirement or alien life exists in outer space?" EBRI found that Americans overwhelmingly sided with Social Security over UFOs by a whopping margin of 71 percent to 26 percent. (Even among Generation X, respondents aged 33 or younger, the margin remained a stunning 63 percent to 33 percent).

Third Millennium not only misrepresented its results on UFOs and Social Security but also recounted an old story about public opinion. Confidence in Social Security's future has been low since the late 1970s.[19]

But, these scholars say, "Despite their low confidence, the public's support has remained strong, according to available trend data."[20]

Another group directing its appeal to the young is Sam Beard's "Economic Security 2000." Beard spreads his message using money from wealthy donors such as Teresa Heinz, the widow of former Senator John Heinz (heir to the Heinz food fortune, a Republican from Pennsylvania, and reportedly the wealthiest man in the Senate at the time of his tragic death in an accident), Cleveland businessman Peter Lewis, and Bob Galvin, Motorola executive. Beard's message is that privatization would enable a worker earning a mere $8,000 per year to retire with almost a half million dollars in investments. It takes little imagination to recognize how imaginative is the math (not to mention the other assumptions) behind his calculations. Beard, by the way, likes to portray himself as a "liberal," because he once worked for Robert Kennedy;[21] under that reasoning, Kennedy himself could be classed as a conservative because he once worked for Senator Joseph McCarthy.

The J. M. Kaplan Fund and the Stuart and John M. Olin Foundations have poured thousands of dollars into anti–Social

Security groups. The Investment Company Institute (ICI) similarly has made lavish campaign contribution to members of Congress. One of Cato's strongest supporters is the brokerage firm of Alex Brown and Sons. Its employees have made large contributions to members of Congress, including those who might be expected to resist weakening Social Security such as Barbara Mikulski, a Democratic senator from Maryland.[22]

Senator Robert Kerrey, Democrat from Nebraska, has been one of the loudest voices calling for "reform." ICI has made contributions to Kerrey and has even had him as keynote speaker for one of their conventions. President Clinton appointed Kerrey to chair the Bipartisan Commission on Entitlement and Tax Reform—apparently as the price of Kerrey's support for the 1993 budget, with its tax increase.[23] That budget passed by a razor-thin majority which contained not a single Republican vote. Its passage was fortunate. It has contributed substantially to the achievement of a balanced budget and should demonstrate clearly to the anti-tax zealots that, contrary to their predictions, a thriving economy is not dependent upon tax cuts. Kerrey can take pride in his vote, however reluctant he was to cast it. It remains to be seen whether Kerrey, whose positions tend to be somewhat erratic, will recognize that flirting with privatizers spells danger for Social Security.

The Cato Institute is one of the most energetic and candid opponents of Social Security, reflecting the institute's libertarian commitment to none but minimal government—regardless of the consequences. Cato has employed José Piñera, former labor minister of Chile, to speak around the country touting the Chilean privatized plan as a model for the United States. "Workers can become capitalists!" is his refrain. For a time, contributions to Chile's system did indeed bring a high rate of return, but in 1995 its returns were a *negative* 2.5 percent. Moreover, the administrative costs are astronomical by the standards of American Social Security, which costs less than 1 percent of income to administer. Chile's administrative fees have recently improved, but still absorb 13 percent.[24] The gigantic and sophisticated United States economy would be well advised not to copy a system that dates only from 1981, is notorious for the large percentage of Chileans who simply fail to participate, is operating in a relatively tiny third-world country under conditions vastly different from those in the United States, and in any case is not working nearly as well as Social Security.

Cato's efforts to portray its paid spokesman as objective are only a small part of its extensive Project on Social Security Privatization. The director of this project is Michael Tanner. It also includes William Shipman of State Street Global Advisors—of Boston's State Street Bank—which has financed extensive advertising in favor of privatization.

In 1997 on a panel in Kansas City, I debated the issues with Tanner and pointed out that Cato had a two million dollar propaganda campaign to undermine Social Security. He corrected me smugly—and proudly.

The figure, he said, was *three* million dollars.

With the great diversity of American news media, one would have expected some skepticism about the sudden announcements of impending doom to a program that has been so successful for so long. Instead, with rare exceptions, the media have accepted the propaganda uncritically. Even worse, many have reported this special-interest propaganda as if they have uncovered it as "news."

Michael Tanner candidly comments that the media have been "very sympathetic." It would be difficult to argue with him on that point. It is distressing to see newspapers simply running Concord Coalition faxes as editorials or op-ed pieces. Concord executive director Martha Phillips has acknowledged happily that "the *Baltimore Sun* ran one on Medicare practically verbatim. Concord's DebtBusters game shows up on newspaper editorial pages." She says, "We like the *Washington Post* editorials today." At the beginning of Concord's campaign, "they weren't singing our tune." After meetings with the *Post*'s staff, though, "it's like they're reading right out of our playbook."[25]

One of the worst purveyors of the propaganda has been the *Kansas City Star*, which not only ran the coalition's Debt-Busters game but used it as an exercise for high schools. To look merely at one example, the *Star*'s deputy editorial page editor often writes as if he were a coalition official. Certainly he accepts their positions without question.

In alleging that there really is no budget surplus, this editor wrote: "How should the big federal entitlement programs—Social Security and Medicare—be reformed?" He answered his own question by proclaiming that "The Concord Coalition has the solution: A new edition of its handy booklet, '10 Questions Voters Should Ask Their Candidates.' The free booklet," he wrote, "includes not only suggested questions but clear, concise explanations of the key budget issues." He went on to say that "the Concord Coalition is a national, non-partisan organization that provides information about the federal budget to the public and advocates fiscal responsibility in Washington," and he urged voters to obtain the booklet by calling the coalition. He published both local and national telephone numbers for the coalition, and went on to say:

> Again, the booklet exposes a big statistical lie: the notion that the Social Security system, without any changes, has enough money set aside to pay benefits until the year 2032. The real trouble is actually only 15 years away.
>
> The Concord Coalition supports means-testing federal benefits to reduce government support for people with middle and high incomes. That's a good, simple solution.
>
> But the "10 Questions" booklet also provides balanced information on other Social Security reforms under discussion, including proposals to raise the retirement age, to lower the annual cost-of-living adjustments, and to "privatize" part of the system.[26]

It seems the Concord Coalition benefits as much from gulli-
bility as from its vast expenditures.

The *Star* did once run opposing op-ed pieces on Social Security from Tanner and me. Otherwise it has been notably reluctant to let commentary favorable to Social Security onto its
editorial pages. Officials from the Social Security Administration tell me that they have tried repeatedly, and unsuccessfully, to persuade the *Star* to print their corrections to some of
the more outrageous misrepresentations that have graced *Star*
editorials.

When *New York Times* reporter Robert Pear wrote an extensive piece quoting economist Dean Baker in praise of Social
Security, the *Pittsburgh Post-Gazette* ran the story. When it
appeared in Pear's own paper, though, the *Times* had cut all
references to Baker and his criticism of those who would undermine Social Security. As Baker says, "The media have
closed off discussion."[27]

To its credit, the *Times* did publish a superb article in its
business section by one of its own editors, Fred Brock, asking
"Save Social Security? From What?"[28] He remarked that when
the new Congress assembled in 1999, it would be tackling the
issue of Social Security. "Politicians talk crisis and issue dire
warnings about the graying of America and the threat of generational warfare," he wrote. "Journalists toss off phrases like
'looming insolvency.' There is little wonder that a survey this
year showed that 68 percent of Americans think that 'fixing'
Social Security is very important."

In striking contrast to nearly all other reports, however,
Brock then pointed out that the system, even under the most
pessimistic forecasts regarding economic growth, is "rock
solid for the next 30 years or so—and, with some minimal
changes, for 40 years after that."

Under more likely scenarios, "even if economic growth
over the next 75 years slows to half the annual average of 3.5
percent over the past 75 years, the Social Security system will
do just fine." This, he said, was the view of Mark Weisbrot, re-

search director of a Washington think tank and coauthor with
Dean Baker of a forthcoming book (with an excellent title),
Social Security: The Phony Crisis. Brock quoted Weisbrot as
saying that "the most important thing we could do to protect
Social Security right now is to leave it alone."

Why then, Brock asked, has there been such a fuss? "Think
hidden agendas," he answered,

> on all sides. Wall Street would love to get its hands on at least
> some of the billions of dollars in the Social Security trust fund.
> And many ultra-conservative Republicans want to privatize the
> system fully. But knowing that the idea won't fly politically,
> they are pushing for partial privatization, in which individuals
> would invest a portion of their contributions in the stock mar-
> ket, all in the name of rescuing the system.

Brock quoted Weisbrot as saying that there is "a kind of
gentlemen's agreement" in Washington not to acknowledge
the "basic fact that we don't really need to be talking about
Social Security." The whole notion of generational conflict,
he argued, is purely a "smoke screen." In 2020, he said, the
median age of the country will have risen from today's thirty-
five, but only to thirty-eight—and that currently is the median age in Florida. The aging of the population will come
slowly, and in any case younger people want their elderly rela-
tives to "have a secure retirement."

Brock's article cuts through the lavishly-financed propaganda barrage. As heartening as it may be to find it in the
country's newspaper of record, it is more disheartening to discover how little the ideas it contained have influenced the editorial policy of the paper that published it, the *Times.* In the
very same issue, the lead editorial remarked that, "the next
Congress will have to deal with nothing less than shoring up
the global economy and devising a plan to save Social Security
in the next generation."[29]

When the *Washington Post* did run an op-ed piece by Henry
Aaron, an economist from the Brookings Institution, who pre-

sented evidence that the portrayal in the media of a "crisis" in Social Security was nonsense, Senator Robert Kerrey blasted Aaron in the pages of the *Congressional Record*.

Television network news is no better. In general, the media seem to have concluded that there is nothing to say about Social Security except to speculate about the proper ways to "save" it. Tanner has crowed that Social Security's supporters were caught "flat-footed," and that the debate is over; the public is convinced that Social Security cannot survive as it is.[30]

Although Tanner overstates his case, it is now commonplace to hear that Social Security unfairly transfers wealth to the elderly from the rest of us, or that it is a "middle-class" entitlement. Previously it was considered—correctly—to be a program that protected nearly the entire population, regardless of age or class. Defining the middle class, or the elderly, as a "special interest," the opponents command attention when they demand that Social Security incorporate a means test (or as Peterson would have it, an "affluence test") to limit it to those who "need" it. A few examples from one year alone, 1993, are illustrative of the concerted campaign against Social Security—and the campaign certainly has not weakened since then.

The "middle-class entitlement" theme was the substance of a representative attack, an article by Lawrence A. Benenson in the *Christian Science Monitor* for 16 February. The title was "Many Retirees Don't Want Aid." Benenson asserted that he had enough money without getting any more "from the government." He had already received more, he said, than he had paid in. He attacked the American Association of Retired Persons (AARP) for its support of Social Security, although he carefully identified himself as a member. Payments to people who do not need them, he argued, were "immoral." Another of his criticisms was that he received more than a welfare mother. This, of course, is irrelevant. It says nothing about Social Security, although it may speak volumes about the welfare system.

Consider a more widely distributed component of the campaign against Social Security, as seen in an article by Jack Anderson with an eye-catching title, "Why Should I Pay For People Who Don't Need It?"[31] Anderson's article was one of several attacks on Social Security in recent years that have appeared in *Parade* magazine, the Sunday supplement. Anderson wrote that a declining number of workers will be supporting an increasing number of retirees. Moreover, he said, "Social Security is not a 'trust fund.'" Of course, that depends upon what he meant. The trust funds are invested in government securities, and they do, indeed, need to be paid back. The same is true for government funds invested in private markets. To say that there is no money in the trust funds, as noted previously, is precisely the same as saying that a safety deposit box has no "money" in it if it is full of government bonds. Anderson called for investment of the trust funds in private securities.

Without acknowledging the source of his ideas, Anderson echoed the calls from the 1960s by Reagan and Goldwater to convert Social Security into a private system. As with his predecessors, he disregarded coverage for disability, Medicare, and survivors. Oddly, Anderson destroyed much of his own case by admitting that "Social Security neither has caused our financial woes nor is it leading us to bankruptcy."

One of the more strident examples in 1993 of the undeclared war on Social Security was a *Newsweek* article by Rich Thomas.[32] Because he recognized that "entitlement" had become a pejorative term, Thomas included Social Security in the same discussion with other "entitlements," although it is totally different. He referred to "the elderly on social security, the poor on food stamps, the sick on Medicare or Medicaid," but carefully avoided mentioning that Social Security is self-supporting and runs a comfortable surplus. He did admit that "some entitlements are more worthy than others. The aging poor need social security," he wrote, "the aging rich do not."

No one has explained why "need" should be a factor, although it has a superficial plausibility. As we have discussed previously, a major reason for Social Security's success is that it in fact does include virtually everyone and that it pays benefits by right, not need. The requirement to undergo humiliating means tests to receive benefits would cause political support for the program to dwindle rapidly and die.

And no wonder. Everyone would continue to pay into the system, but only a minority would receive benefits. Would that be equitable? When support dried up, so would the program. It would die, and that is exactly the goal of its opponents. A retired executive may not "need" his or her corporate pension, but no one suggests easing the burden on corporations by withdrawing it. A wealthy widow might not "need" the proceeds of her husband's life-insurance policy, but no one suggests relieving the company on that account of its obligation to pay—even if it is in trouble, which the Social Security system (apart from possible difficulties facing Medicare, to be discussed in Chapter 8) is not.

Although my main topic is Social Security, I must respond to articles such as Thomas's, that the other entitlements are also valuable to the social fabric of this country. The rising cost of Medicaid is one of the more plausible economic threats. Do we merely cut it? "Yes," said Rich Thomas. At what cost?—the removal of medical care for the poor. Cut food stamps? "Yes," said Thomas. At what cost?—lessening the amount of food for the poor.

Is this the only answer for our wealthy society? Aggravating their plight damages more than the poor. It threatens the middle and upper classes also, we who progressively retreat into the suburbs, behind our security systems, and fear for our children, if not for ourselves. Encouraging social unrest is short-sighted policy that does not help us economically or otherwise. It could easily be the greatest threat of all to "family values."

In any case, whatever the attitudes toward the other entitlements may be, the public—appropriately—continues to
see Social Security in a different light. The barrage of anti–
Social Security propaganda and uncritical media coverage of
the issue has resulted in some loss of confidence, but fortunately the reality of the public's attitude is not so simple as
Social Security's enemies would wish. Despite their off-the-
cuff answers, people do seem to believe that they will receive
Social Security. The same polls that report loss of confidence
in Social Security also report that more than 90 percent of
the respondents expect it to be a significant source of their
retirement income. Results from focus groups conducted
over a decade reveal that early in the group discussions, people often said "matter-of-factly that Social Security would
not 'be there' in the future. Later, having the groups talk
about Social Security forced people to think about what they
were saying." Frequently, their attitudes changed as it "became clear that the matter-of-fact 'it won't be there' statement was not based on any sort of judgment. It was simply a
reaction."[33]

Change in Public Understanding
of Social Security

The public once understood Social Security quite well and
probably continues to understand it better than its opponents
would wish. Many misconceptions, though, do now prevail.
Some, to be sure, may result from the increasingly complex
nature of the programs, but in large part they stem from deliberate efforts to undermine social insurance in the United
States. After many years, the underground grumbling of those
who believe that the government has no place in ensuring the
welfare of its citizens, riding the success of Reaganism, coalesced into a persistent campaign against one of the most popular and beneficial programs this country has ever enacted.

How different all this negativity about Social Security is from the atmosphere that existed when I went to work for the Social Security Administration as a young management intern in 1959. After running out of funds, I was faced almost literally with the prospect of becoming a starving graduate student and therefore found it a distinct pleasure to accept the position in Baltimore at the headquarters of Social Security. I even accepted the status of "government bureaucrat." Despite the somewhat cynical attitude that I brought with me from the academic world, I was impressed with much that I found. SSA was widely accepted as a model government agency. Its employees, from the lowest to the highest, prided themselves on providing service to the public and had no doubt that they deserved to be considered as top-notch. Certainly things were far from perfect, but the employees were dedicated and efficient, and prided themselves on humanizing an enormous bureaucracy.[34]

The public, too, accepted Social Security with pride as an earned benefit, not a "handout." It was not "welfare," but had become part of the "American Way of Life." Brochures from SSA explaining the program even stressed that actor and comedian Eddie Cantor had qualified for benefits in one month in which he had no earnings, although he was a millionaire and earned large amounts in other months that year. If even he could apply, surely there could be no stigma involved. The agency made strenuous efforts to seek out those who were eligible and to ensure that they received benefits.

The cuts of the 1980s came long after I had left government service in the 1960s. The Social Security Administration became a target of Social Security's opponents. Eroding the Agency was one way of attacking Social Security without arousing public ire. Morale plummeted, as employees became overworked and underappreciated. When letters brought tardy or no response, telephones went unanswered, or claims took seemingly interminable time to process, the public was encouraged to blame "government bureaucrats," not the elected officials who for twelve years worked directly and diligently to undermine Social Security in the United States. There has been improvement since the 1980s, but even though Social Security programs are far larger now than in the 1960s, SSA still has far fewer employees than it did then. Today, if we listen to the remnants of the mean-spirited 1980s, we would be forced to conclude that the primary job of such an agency is to move heaven and earth not in order to provide benefits to those who are eligible, but to deny them to those who are not.

We should remember that in the view of Social Security's enemies, those "who are not eligible" would AND SHOULD include nearly all of us! The central figure among those enemies was Ronald Regan. Just how striking a departure from tradition his role was becomes even clearer when we consider his predecessors.

The role of American presidents has been crucial in developing and maintaining Social Security. Their support was uniform from FDR through Jimmy Carter and included Republicans as well as Democrats. In the next chapter I will take a close look at the language they used to support Social Security and contrast it to Reagan's language as he attacked and sought to undermine the entire notion of social insurance.

Presidential Attitudes Toward Social Security

Only Desperate Men with Their Backs to the Wall

The individualistic nature of American thought and traditions often lead to antigovernmental tendencies. These tendencies can make it difficult for the government to act positively. They place fewer restraints on the power of the government to act negatively—they can even encourage it. This is especially so with regard to the government's major actor, the president.

The power of a president to restrain action, to reduce programs, to slow movement, or to keep things as they are is considerably greater than the power to expand existing programs or to innovate. In both cases, the president's personality and ability to command a following are crucial, but never more so than when the attempt is to produce positive, as opposed to negative, action. Executive appeals to the public have become a vital part of America's political process, and to be successful those appeals must be crafted with sensitivity to the values and symbols of American politic.

Social Security, as great a departure from tradition as any program in American political history, is a case in point. It was necessary first to tailor the program to fit American conditions and needs, and then to demonstrate how its departure from tradition enhanced, rather than violated, American values. By any measure the programs that the Social Security Act of 1935 created and inspired are among the most ambitious and successful activities ever undertaken by the American political system—or by any political system anywhere. Presidential rhetoric alone can accomplish little or nothing, but it was a key ingredient both in Social Security's implementation and in the dramatic expansion of coverage and benefits. It also has been crucial in conditioning the attitudes of Americans to this program, which has been not only highly popular, despite the fact that it is strikingly inconsistent with American attitudes of individualism as traditionally interpreted.

Much of the credit for the initial wide acceptance of Social Security must go to Franklin D. Roosevelt for the brilliant manner in which he used traditional American rhetoric to associate the Social Security Act with American values and to defend it against charges that it was alien and foreign. "One of the most interesting features of the acceptance speeches of President Carter and Governor Reagan in 1980," for instance, "was their dispute about who should be able to claim the mantle of Franklin Roosevelt."[1] Roosevelt set the tone, and at least until Reagan his successors have followed his lead, through good times and bad, both reflecting and generating popular support.

Roosevelt's artistry in the use of political rhetoric, his ability to meld change with continuity in a nonthreatening manner, was extraordinary. Take, for example, his famous "Four Freedoms" declaration. Freedom, of course, had been the central tenet of America's political ideology at least since the Revolution. Thus, he was thoroughly in accord with the country's tradition when he proclaimed as central to his program the "freedom of speech" and the "freedom of religion." When he proceeded to add "freedom from want" and "freedom from fear," however, he was enlarging upon that tradition. He added "two parts security under the label of 'freedom'" to the idea of freedom in the "classic liberal sense."[2]

Roosevelt's skill at using rhetoric to bring support for innovation without discarding the traditional characterized his approach to the New Deal in general and to the Social Security Act in particular. "Even the most precedent-breaking New Deal projects reflected capitalist thinking and deferred to business sensibilities. Social Security was modeled, often irrelevantly, on private-insurance systems."[3] By including private insurance principles in the Social Security Act, it was possible to lessen the burden of individual responsibility without doing violence to traditional beliefs regarding the place of the individual and the role of government.

There was also another political reason. It is well known that Roosevelt wished the program to be designed in such a manner as to protect it from future politicians who might be tempted to reduce or eliminate it. The "insurance-company model" would create within the public a sense of ownership, and a separate trust fund would protect both the program—since such a trust fund would be visible and call attention to any attacks upon it—and the general treasury.[4] He made his intention clear in a speech in New York a year after the adoption of the Social Security Act.

Speaking at Madison Square Garden on 31 October 1936, in response to the well-orchestrated "pay-envelope campaign," the president said:

> Only desperate men with their backs to the wall would descend so far below the level of decent citizenship as to foster the current pay-envelope campaign against America's working people. [Boos]. . . . They tell the worker that his wage will be reduced by a contribution to some vague form of old-age insurance. But they carefully conceal from him the fact that for every dollar of premium he pays for that insurance, the employer pays another dollar. That omission is deceit. . . .
>
> But they are guilty of more than deceit. When they imply that the reserves thus created . . . will be stolen by some future Congress—diverted to some wholly foreign purpose, they attack the integrity and honor of American Government itself. Those who

suggest that, are already aliens to the spirit of American democracy. Let them emigrate and try their lot under some foreign flag in which they have more confidence. [Applause][5]

Roosevelt thus reassured Americans as to the safety of Social Security, and he also warned future politicians against attempts to divert funds from the program. He also managed at the same time to describe an attack upon a government program as an attack, not upon government, but upon "working people." Additionally, his rhetoric was strictly conventional. Americans understood "premiums," "insurance policies," and even "contributions." Such language is thoroughly consistent with private enterprise, and sounds in no manner as if it is "socialistic," "alien," or even governmental. In fact, in adopting language that assumed that the programs under the act were "American" in character, Roosevelt was able to turn the tables upon the opponents and associate them with forces alien "to the spirit of American democracy." He thus linguistically symbolized a government innovation as an outgrowth of American tradition and suggested that those who opposed it were the ones under foreign influence.

Although the tone was of course different, Roosevelt's rhetoric describing the program itself remained consistent with his comments upon signing the Social Security Act more than a year earlier, on 14 August 1935. At that time he had spoken of protection for citizens whose lives, because of industrial changes, had tended more to become insecure, conceding that it would never be possible to insure the entire population against all of the "hazards and vicissitudes of life." He referred to the beginnings of Social Security as a "corner stone in a structure which is being built but is by no means complete," and described the program as one that also would be beneficial to the country's economy. It would protect "the Government against the necessity of going deeply into debt to furnish relief to the needy," and would provide "a law to flatten out the peaks and valleys of deflation and of inflation—in other words, a law that will take care of human needs and at the same time provide for the United States an economic structure of vastly greater soundness."[6]

The themes that Roosevelt sounded were outgrowths of ideas that he had long advocated. In August 1931, he spoke as governor to the New York Legislature, saying that the government must extend aid to the unemployed "not as a matter of charity but as a matter of social duty."[7] Previously, in discussing a New York pension bill, he had asserted that "our American aged do not want charity." Rather, he said, they seek "old age comforts to which they are rightfully entitled by their own thrift and foresight in the form of insurance." As for the bill itself, "we can only hope," he said, "that this will be a forerunner of a proper system of security against old-age want in the years to come."[8] When he accepted the Democratic nomination for president in 1932, he cited "work and security" as prime goals of the party. Somewhat more than a year later, he declared that security for individuals and families would be the foremost objective of his administration and called for social insurance as the mechanism to provide it, with funds to be contributed by workers and employers to a program that would be national in scope.[9]

So effective has Roosevelt's rhetoric been in influencing both public policy and public attitudes, that it can be difficult to recognize the extent to which his views were different—strikingly different—from those preceding him. President Hoover, for example, prior to his presidency had fully earned a reputation as a humanitarian by his effective organization of food distribution to areas devastated by the First World War. Nevertheless, as president he vetoed a bill to provide federal relief for unemployment, saying "never before has so dangerous a suggestion been seriously made in this country."[10]

By the State of the Union message of 1935, Roosevelt's emphasis on security and reform had become so strong that Basil Rauch saw in his policies the beginnings of a second New

Deal.[11] His rhetoric had stressed "the average man," in a reference to William Graham Sumner's "The Forgotten Man," to demonstrate that the New Deal indeed had not forgotten ordinary people. By the time of his second inaugural address, however, FDR's emphasis had expanded to include those who were far lower than average. Achieving a poetic flair, he said that he saw "one third of a nation ill-housed, ill-clad, ill-nourished," and added that "we are determined to make every American citizen the subject of his country's interest and concern; and we will never regard any faithful, law-abiding group within our borders as superfluous."[12] He clearly and directly stated the new obligations of government in his State of the Union address in 1938, when he said that "Government has a final responsibility for the well-being of its citizenship."[13] Such a conception, announced so directly, could only have been startling a few brief years earlier. By 1938, however, the public was receptive, partly—perhaps in large part—because of Roosevelt's skillful nurturing of the idea.

Nevertheless, at no time did Roosevelt fail to pay homage to traditional values or to associate his innovations with those values. In the fifth State of the Union message of his presidency, on the third of January that year, Roosevelt demonstrated that his rhetorical skill remained undiminished and that he had not lost sight of the need to keep his ties to American values. "As a nation," he said, "we have rejected any radical revolutionary program. For a permanent correction of grave weaknesses in our economic system we have relied on new applications of old democratic processes."[14] He thus demonstrated the validity of the observation that in order to implement an innovation, a president must describe the new program, however radical a departure from traditional values it may be, as the embodiment of those values.

Despite the pressures of the Second World War, Roosevelt did not let preoccupation with the conflict cause him to forget domestic social issues. On 5 February 1944, he held a press conference at the White House for the Negro Newspaper Publishers Association. He declared himself to be "for extension of the system of social security, which recognizes the right of the individual to self-development, protection against the hazards of illness, unemployment and want, and promotes the orderly development of the nation's resources."[15]

He kept the rhetoric alive. In a campaign speech in Washington later that year on 23 September before the Teamsters, he accused the Republicans of appropriating that rhetoric. "I got quite a laugh," he said, "when I read this plank in the Republican platform . . . 'The Republican party accepts the purposes of the National Labor Relations Act, the Wage and Hour Act, the Social Security Act and all other Federal statutes designed to promote and protect the welfare of American working men and women, and we promise a fair and just administration of these laws.'" His comments provoked laughter, and he proceeded to charge the Republicans with having worked to fight each of those programs, saying that they "would not even recognize these progressive laws, if they met them in broad daylight."[16] The laughter continued.

Although FDR's successor as president, Harry S Truman, made no effort to duplicate Roosevelt's rhetorical heights, his language reflected the same themes. Certainly he was fully his predecessor's equal in the strong support that he provided for Social Security and in his efforts to expand the minimal program that the New Deal had provided. In his combative manner, he continued to associate Social Security with insurance and to stress its beneficial effects. In 1948, for example, in speaking before the Greater Los Angeles Press Club on 14 June, he said:

> I've been asking the Congress to broaden the base of Social Security so more people could benefit from the Social Security Act. . . .
>
> Now, do you know how Congress has broadened the base of Social Security? They've just taken 750,000 people off Social Security and sent me a bill to that effect and tied a rider onto it in-

creasing the old-age assistance, hoping I'd take the bait and let them get away with tearing up Social Security. I didn't do it. I vetoed that bill this morning. I've told the Congress that if they would pass the bill in the proper form I'd be happy to sign it, and they have plenty of time to pass it in the proper form—don't think they haven't.[17]

In the same talk he called for a major addition, one unprecedented in the United States and affecting the average citizen: "I wish the Congress would go into this health situation and pass an intelligent health bill for the benefit of the whole country, so that everybody could get medical care at a reasonable price when he needs it. . . . There are only two classes of people who can get the proper medical care nowadays, and that is the indigent and the very rich."[18] His proposal, of course, elicited tremendous opposition and was not seriously considered.

Truman missed no opportunity to call for expansion of Social Security benefits. In his State of the Union message on 5 January 1949, shortly after his reelection, he said:

The Government has still other opportunities—to help raise the standard of living of our citizens. These opportunities lie in the fields of social security, health, education, housing and civil rights.

The present coverage of the social security laws is altogether inadequate, and benefit payments are too low. One third of our workers are not covered. Those who receive old age and survivors insurance benefits receive an average payment of only $25 a month. Many others who cannot work because they are physically disabled are left to the mercy of charity.

We should expand our social security program, both as to the size of the benefits and extent of coverage, against the economic hazards due to unemployment, old age, sickness, and disability.

We must spare no effort to raise the general level of health in this country. In a nation as rich as ours, it is a shocking fact that tens of millions lack adequate medical care. We are short of doctors, hospitals, and nurses. We must remedy these shortages. Moreover, we need—and we must have without further delay— a system of pre-paid medical insurance which will enable every American to afford good medical care.[19]

Although the style differed, the populist spirit that had infused Roosevelt's rhetoric remained. So did the spirit of innovation and the stress on the average citizen's need. At least by implication, Truman's rhetoric also continued Roosevelt's association of social insurance with American values and traditions. In fact, in countering his critics, he explicitly raised the issue of rhetoric. For example, in a speech at the Allegheny County Fair in Pittsburgh on 5 September 1949, he belligerently attacked those who opposed social welfare and the expansion of Social Security:

These propagandists do not argue the merits of our program. They know that the American people will always decide against the selfish interests if all the facts are before them. So they have adopted an age-old device to hide the weakness of their case.

This is the device of the "scare word" campaign.

It is a device that has been used in every country and every age by the propagandists for selfish interests. They invent slogans in an effort to scare the people. They apply frightening labels to anything they happen to oppose. These scare words are intended to confuse the people and turn them against their own best interests.

Scare words change with the times.

When Franklin Delano Roosevelt and the New Deal saved our country from the great depression, the selfish interests raised the scare words of "socialism" and "regimentation."

But the American people didn't scare.

Year after year the selfish interests kept up their refrain. They tried new words—"bureaucracy" and "bankruptcy."

But the American people still didn't scare.

Last November the people gave the selfish interests the surprise of their lives. The people just didn't believe that programs designed to assure them decent housing, adequate wages, improved medical care, and better education were "socialism" or "regimentation."

So, the selfish interests retired to a back room with their high-priced advertising experts and thought things over. They decided that the old set of scare words had become a little mildewed. Maybe it was time for a change.

So they came up with a new set of scare words. Now they're talking about "collectivism," and "statism," and "the welfare state."

The selfish interests don't know—and in fact they don't care—what these words mean. They're using those words only because they want to turn the American people against the programs which the people want, and need, and for which the people voted. . . .

The people want a better social security system, improved education, and a national health program. The selfish interests are trying to sabotage these programs because they have no concern about helping the little fellow, and so they call this the "welfare state."

Well, we don't care what they call it.[20]

By describing the rhetoric of his opponents as empty propaganda, Truman attempted to establish clearly that government programs to assist citizens economically were indeed consistent with individualism, freedom, and a limited state. It is noteworthy that at this time public fear of "socialism" and government programs was joining with apprehension regarding the expansion of Marxism-Leninism to produce the beginnings of what soon came to be called McCarthyism.

Truman continued such themes—and his belligerency—throughout his presidency. Speaking before a political group at a Jefferson-Jackson Day dinner in Washington in March 1952, he announced that he would not be a candidate for reelection, and he attacked what he called the "dinosaur school of Republican strategy." Those of the "dinosaur school," he argued, were saying, "Let's stop beating about the bush—let's

say what we really believe. Let's say we're against social security—and we're against the labor unions and good wages. . . .
—that we're against the Government doing anything for any-
body except big business." Truman conceded that he had
some sympathy for this group, because they were urging their
party to tell the truth, but that their prescription would not be
good for the country or for their party, which in response to
the truth would receive only the "dinosaur vote."

Rather than the "dinosaur strategy," he said, the Republicans would adopt a "white is black" campaign. "First of all
they will try to make people believe that everything the Government has done for this country is socialism. They will go
to the people and say: 'Did you see that Social Security check
you received the other day—you thought that was good for
you, didn't you? That's nothing in the world but socialism.'"[21]

Such rhetoric may have helped to protect Social Security, if
protection indeed were needed at the time for such a popular
program. It may even have helped in bringing about an expansion of coverage in 1950 to include most of the self-employed,
and the increases of benefits in 1951 and 1952. It did not,
however, appreciably advance the fortunes of Truman's proposal for health care, nor did it prevent the strong Republican
victory in 1952 that brought General Dwight D. Eisenhower
to the White House.

Far from being a disaster for Social Security, however, the
Republican victory showed just how much a part of the American way of life Social Security had become. Eisenhower assumed the presidency at the height of McCarthyism, during a
time of growth and prosperity. It could have been a time conducive to an attack on Social Security, but Eisenhower continued the pattern of support set by his two predecessors, differ-
ing essentially only in emphasis. He accepted Social Security,
even though he did add a "Yes, but" note.

For example, as a candidate he ran against "too much government." His "middle way," he said ". . . assumes that all
Americans of all parties have now accepted and will forever

support what we call social gains, the security that people are entitled to in their old age and to make certain that they are adequately cared for, insured against unemployment, equal opportunities for everybody regardless of race, religion, where he was born or what is his national origin." He said that social gains were to provide a solid floor, "But on top of that floor, let's not interfere with the incentive, the ambition, the right of any of you to build the most glorious structure on top of that floor you can imagine."[22] The rhetoric thus continued the language combining individualism with support for Social Security, but added a note of caution. Despite the cautionary note, it is plain that the Republican Party had accepted Social Security.

Eisenhower did not mention Social Security in his inaugural address on 20 January 1953.[23] The following month, however, in his first State of the Union message, he adopted rhetoric that could have come from Roosevelt or Truman and called for significant expansion of Social Security:

This Administration is profoundly aware of two great needs born of our living in a complex industrial economy. First: the individual citizen must have safeguards against personal disasters inflicted by forces beyond his control. Second: The welfare of the people demands effective and economical performance by the Government of certain indispensable social services.

In the light of this responsibility, certain general purposes and certain concrete measures are plainly indicated now.

There is urgent need for greater effectiveness in our programs, both public and private, offering safeguards against the privations that too often come with unemployment, old age, illness, and accident.

The provisions of the old age and survivors insurance law should promptly be extended to cover millions of citizens who have been left out of the Social Security System.[24]

Eisenhower's proposal made plain that Social Security had become a nonpartisan issue and had indeed been accepted by the polity as a whole. The next year, he again devoted a portion of his State of the Union address to reiterate his call for expansion. His rhetoric describing the system had come to differ little from that of the New Dealers. On 7 January 1954, he said:

> Our basic social security program, the old-age and survivors insurance system, to which individuals contribute during their productive years and receive benefits based on previous earnings, is designed to shield from destitution. Last year I recommended extension of the social insurance system to include more than 10 million additional persons. I ask that this extension soon be accomplished. This and other major improvements in the insurance system will bring substantial benefit increases and broaden the membership of the insurance system, thus diminishing the need for Federal grants-in-aid for such purposes.[25]

He even built into his address a recognition of the inadequacies of the health care system. "I am flatly opposed to the socialization of medicine," he said, and stressed that the needs were best met through private efforts. On the other hand, he noted the rising costs of medical care and the hardships that were resulting. "The Federal Government can do many helpful things," he remarked, "and still avoid the socialization of medicine." Among the things he mentioned were assistance to research and to hospital construction.[26]

In his 1955 State of the Union message, Eisenhower boasted of the "notable advances" in certain "functions of government" during his administration. "Protection of old-age and survivors' insurance was extended to an additional ten million of our people," he said.[27] In the address for the following year, he again noted the extension of coverage and the increase in benefits with pride, and called for yet further expansion:

> Under the 1954 amendments to the old-age and survivors' insurance program protection was extended to some ten million addi-

tional workers and benefits were increased. The system now helps protect nine out of ten American workers and their families against loss of income in old age or on the death of the breadwinner. The system is sound. It must be kept so. In developing improvements in the system we must give the most careful consideration to population and social trends and to fiscal requirements. With these considerations in mind the Administration will present its recommendations for further expansion of coverage and other steps which can be taken wisely at this time.[28]

In his reelection campaign, President Eisenhower continued to speak as glowingly of Social Security as any New Dealer. "We made coverage virtually complete," he said, ". . . and we put through the biggest real increase in benefits in the program's history."[29] It is significant, also, that during the Eisenhower administration came the addition, in 1956, of disability benefits, an enormously important expansion of the Social Security system. Although Eisenhower did not mention Social Security in his Farewell Address,[30] he did take time in his final State of the Union message once again to point out that, "The coverage of the Social Security Act has been broadened since 1953 to make 11,000,000 additional people eligible for retirement, disability or survivors benefits for themselves or their dependents, and the Social Security benefits have been substantially improved."[31]

To be sure, the parties did vary in their emphases, but there can be no doubt that both the Democratic and Republican Parties had accepted Social Security as an American institution.

With the election of John F. Kennedy, despite the pressures of the Cold War, Social Security again was placed at the top of the political agenda, this time in the form of a strong effort to secure passage of health benefits for the elderly. Because of the fervent opposition from many quarters, including among others the insurance industry, the U.S. Chamber of Commerce, the pharmaceutical manufacturers, and—especially—

the American Medical Association, discussed in Chapter 4, Kennedy's program generated a furious rhetorical battle.[32] His language remained firmly within the pattern established by his predecessors, and, following their lead, he used the State of the Union address to call for action. On 11 January 1962, he said to the Congress and the American people that, "in matters of health, no piece of unfinished business is more important or more urgent than the enactment under the social security system of health insurance for the aged." He proceeded to say that "Social security has long helped to meet the hardships of retirement, death, and disability. I now urge that its coverage be extended without further delay to provide health insurance for the elderly."[33] The struggle was under way.

In a major address to the National Council of Senior Citizens in New York on 20 May 1962, Kennedy cited examples of need for government provisions for health care, and said, "We say that during his working years [the worker] will contribute to Social Security, as he has in the case of his retirement." He proceeded to praise physicians, but criticize the proposal's opponents and condemn what he termed the misinformation that they disseminated. He denied that it in any way would interfere with freedom or provide a "handout." He spoke of "great unfinished business in this country," and conceded that "while this bill does not solve our problems in this area, I do not believe it is a valid argument to say this bill isn't going to do the job. It will not, but it will do part of it." He reminded his listeners that "all the great revolutionary movements of the Franklin Roosevelt Administration in the Thirties we now take for granted," and used his trademark metaphor of moving this country forward.[34] Thus Kennedy associated revolutionary (radical) actions with individual freedom. Such rhetoric was congenial to Americans because of their reverence for the American Revolution. The effect was to praise the New Deal's programs and their extensions as supports for individualism.

1962 was a year of stormy controversy, with charges, countercharges, and threats flying back and forth in a rapid and confusing manner. Physicians' groups threatened boycotts, the AMA alleged that what had come to be called "Medicare" would be a "cruel hoax" for the poor, and that the U.S. Treasury was being "looted to help subsidize the biggest lobbying campaign this nation has ever seen" in support of the proposal. In March, Democratic National Chair John M. Bailey called the AMA an "ally of the John Birch Society in a surgical mask."

Kennedy, himself, had commented during a news conference on 23 May that the AMA had been one of the chief opponents of Social Security in the 1930s. AMA President Leonard Larson said that Kennedy's charge was "entirely incorrect," and that the AMA had never taken a position on the legislation. Kennedy retorted by referring to the 1939 *JAMA* editorial that said that "all forms of security, compulsory security, even against old age and unemployment, represent a beginning invasion by the state into the personal life of the individual, represent a taking away of individual responsibility, a weakening of national caliber, a definite step toward either communism or totalitarianism." As noted earlier, the AMA's position was that only resolutions adopted by the association's House of Delegates reflect official AMA policy. To bolster his charges, Kennedy reminded the AMA of the resolution by its House of Delegates in 1949, saying that "so-called 'Social Security'" was in fact "socialism," that it had failed everywhere it had been tried, and that it always "served as the entering wedge for establishment of a socialistic form of government control over the lives and fortunes of the people."[35]

Kennedy had devoted a huge amount of effort to Medicare's passage. His assassination did not diminish the effort. Lyndon B. Johnson made Medicare, along with aid to education, civil rights, and a general "war on poverty," top priorities in his new administration.

In his State of the Union message on 8 January 1964, Johnson said:

> Let this session of Congress be known . . . as the session which declared all-out war on human poverty and unemployment in these United States; as the session which finally recognized the health needs of all of our older citizens. . . . We must provide hospital insurance for our older citizens financed by every worker and his employer under Social Security . . . to protect him in his old age in a dignified manner, without cost to the treasury, against the devastating hardship of prolonged or repeated illness. . . . Every American will benefit by the extension of Social Security to cover the hospital costs of their aged parents.[36]

Thus he launched the battle by adopting a ringing martial rhetoric incorporating the same symbols employed by Roosevelt at the beginning of Social Security: dignity, unmet needs, financing by workers without strain to the treasury, and widespread benefit to all. He included strong reference to Social Security in his speech accepting the 1964 Democratic nomination in Atlantic City, portraying it as a mainstay of human freedom. "Most Americans," he said, "want medical care for older citizens, and so do I. . . . For more than 30 years, from Social Security to the war against poverty, we have diligently worked to enlarge the freedom of man."[37]

Johnson's opponent that year was Senator Barry Goldwater, who represented the most conservative wing of the Republican Party. For the first time since the 1930s, comments from a major party's presidential candidate led to concern that he might, if elected, move to make Social Security a voluntary system, thus changing it completely, and—most experts believed—destroying it. Goldwater went down to a crushing defeat, as Johnson won by a popular-vote margin unexcelled in American history. Most observers believed that the perception that Goldwater was hostile to Social Security was one of several major factors in his defeat.

Johnson won his victory with nurturing rhetoric, such as "we seek to care for the old through medical care under Social Security."[38] He continued his approach after the election, and again on 4 January 1965 devoted time in his State of the Union message to the subject. He adopted rhetorical symbols of justice, dignity, and struggle. "Let a just nation," he said, "promise: To the elderly . . . hospital care under Social Security and . . . raising benefit payments to those struggling to maintain the dignity of their later years."[39]

The Congress responded to Johnson's patient and determined urging. After years of effort by dedicated supporters, Congress adopted legislation adding Medicare to the Social Security system, but Johnson did not stop. In his State of the Union message in 1967 he boasted of bringing "medical care to older people," and said that "three and one-half million Americans have already received treatment under Medicare since July." Nevertheless, he said, "we should raise Social Security payments," and "I will ask that you raise the minimum payment by 59 per cent . . . and to guarantee a minimum benefit of $100 a month for those with a total of 25 years of coverage." Furthermore, "we should extend Medicare benefits that are now denied to 1,300,000 permanently and totally disabled Americans under 65 years of age."[40]

Throughout his presidency, Johnson continued to point with pride to the many people who had received treatment through Medicare. He also faulted those who had been in opposition, especially Republicans. "In the Congress," he said, "some closed their ears and their ranks" to the need. "93 per cent of the House Republicans voted to kill the Medicare Bill."[41] In his 1968 State of the Union address on 17 January, he boasted that "last year, Medicare, Medicaid and other new programs brought better health to more than 25 million Americans."[42] The Great Society programs, Medicare, civil rights, aid to education, and the War on Poverty were LBJ's fondest accomplishments even as the Vietnam War wore him down both physically and emotionally, causing him to relinquish the presidency.

In his final State of the Union message, delivered on 14 January 1969, Johnson kept pressing, taking this last opportunity to use careful rhetoric and to craft symbols on behalf of Social Security. He noted that "Medicare, that we were unable to pass for so many years, is now a part of American life." Moreover, "since the enactment of the Social Security Act in 1935, Congress," he said:

has recognized the necessity to 'make more adequate provision for aged persons . . . maternal and child welfare . . . and public health.'
And that is the words of Congress.
The time has come, I think, to make it more adequate and I think we should increase social security benefits and I am so recommending. . . .
Our nation is rightly proud of its medical advances. But we should remember that our country ranks 15th among the nations of the world in its infant mortality rate.
I think we should assure decent medical care for every expectant mother, and for their children during the first year of their life in the United States of America.
I think we should protect our children and their families from the costs of catastrophic illness.[43]

Lyndon B. Johnson must have felt despair when foreign policy not only consumed his administration but diverted the country from his Great Society. Thurgood Marshall and others have mentioned that it destroyed him. Nevertheless, he did not permit any despair he felt to prevent him from presenting a final grand rhetorical picture of a caring country, one that had moved toward his vision of a Great Society, as he relinquished the presidency to his successor, Richard M. Nixon.

President Nixon did not stress Social Security in his inaugural address or his first State of the Union message. On 2 December 1969, however, he startled the country with a plan that in many respects went considerably beyond the Social Security system. At a White House Conference on Food, Nutrition, and Health, although he did not refer specifically to Social Security, Nixon proposed "for the first time, this new Family Assistance Plan" that "would give every American family a basic income. . . ."[44] The plan did not succeed, but it demonstrated that Nixon was willing to speak the same language as his predecessors with regard to social issues.

The Nixon administration in general did not place Social Security in the position of first priority, but when the president spoke of Social Security and related matters, he used the supportive rhetoric that had become more or less traditional. In his State of the Union message on 22 January 1971, for example, Nixon did not stress Social Security, but outlined six "great goals," the fourth of which was to "offer a far-reaching set of proposals for improving America's health care and making it available more fairly to more people. I will propose," he said, "a program to insure that no American family will be prevented from obtaining basic medical care by inability to pay." The program included aid to medical schools, incentives to those who delivered health services, some new encouragements for preventive medicine, and a $100 million effort to fight cancer.[45] Although this was not a Social Security proposal and was not a call for universal health coverage to be guaranteed by the government, the issue was related, and the rhetoric could have been taken directly from speeches on Social Security by earlier presidents.

Similar rhetoric permeated his acceptance speech on 23 August 1972, after receiving renomination. "And while we are talking about welfare," he said, "let us quit treating our senior citizens in this country like welfare recipients. They have worked hard all of their lives to build America. And as the builders of America, they have not asked for a handout. What they ask for is what they have earned—and that is retirement in dignity and self-respect. Let's give that to our senior citizens."[46]

Nixon won the election by a huge landslide, and his victory could hardly have been in doubt. Despite his almost assured victory, he sought assistance from the popularity of Social Security. "A president can judiciously time economic benefits to interest groups or certain segments of the electorate to ensure their support on election day. Timing of Social Security increases provides a classic example of this point. Checks went out in October 1972, one month before the elections, with the following memo enclosed and personally approved by President Nixon to each of the 24.7 million Social Security recipients:

> Your social security payment has been increased by 20% starting with this month's check by a new statute enacted by Congress and signed into law by President Richard Nixon on July 1, 1972.

> The President also signed into law a provision which will allow your social security benefits to increase automatically if the cost of living goes up.

This example from the Nixon administration is hardly unique."[47] The timing of transfer payments to create good will prior to elections is fairly common. It does, however, have a unique aspect.

What makes this instance unusual is that President Nixon had approved the Social Security benefit increase solely because he had no choice: it was attached to a bill that he thought to be essential. He had favored a small increase only, and had threatened to veto the increase that he ultimately signed (and for which he took credit) because he believed it to be too great. It is true that fears of a cash-flow shortage emerged during his administration, which led to a delay of an automatic adjustment of benefits that took place after Nixon left office. Neither the threatened veto nor this delay, however, should be interpreted as reflecting hostility to social insurance.

Regardless of the extent to which Nixon may have lacked enthusiasm for the large Social Security increase, he clearly accepted the Social Security system. His rhetoric was traditionally supportive, and at no time did he demonstrate anything resembling opposition. Like his predecessor Lyndon Johnson, he boasted of increases and system expansion. Speaking over the radio on 24 February 1973, Nixon said, "Social security cash benefits for the elderly and the disabled in fiscal year 1974 will be twice what they were four years ago. Next year, five million additional poor, aged, and disabled persons will receive health benefits."[48] Nixon had joined the succession of presidents—Republican as well as Democrat—who, however their emphases may have varied, accepted and supported the Social Security system and described it with symbolically similar rhetoric.

When Gerald Ford replaced Richard Nixon as president, he followed his predecessors in supporting Social Security and even in calling for expansion and benefit increases. As with some of the others, he did not place matters relating to the program at the top of his agenda. Also, he faced inflation that caused him concern. Accordingly, he sounded an unusual note. In his State of the Union message of 15 January 1975, speaking not exclusively of Social Security, he charged that "we have been self-indulgent. For decades, we have been voting ever-increasing levels of government benefits—and now the bill has come due. . . . One characteristic of these programs is that their cost increases automatically every year because the number of people eligible for most of the benefits increases every year." Ford outlined several cost-cutting mechanisms, and then said, "As an additional step toward putting the Federal Government's house in order, I recommend a 5 percent limit on Federal pay increases in 1975. In all Government programs tied to the Consumer Price Index—including Social Security, Civil Service and military retirement pay, and food stamps—I also propose a one-year maximum increase of 5 percent."[49]

The purpose for imposing ceilings was to combat inflation, but the move suggested that Social Security might at some time face actual reduction because of a budget revision that Lyndon Johnson had inaugurated in 1968. At that time, he and the Congress accepted a recommendation to include receipts and disbursements from "the Social Security, Medicare, highway and other trust funds" with the ordinary budget for purposes of accounting.[50]

The purpose, of course, was to use the substantial excess of income over outgo of the trust funds to reduce the appearance of the budget deficit. It is significant in this regard that 1968 was the last year in which the budget was reported as being balanced until the second term of the Clinton administration. If deficits were to grow, the pressure that held down Social Security increases to counter inflation could for the first time become pressure to reduce benefits in order to reduce the deficit. Certainly, as their rhetoric indicated, neither Johnson, Nixon, Ford, nor, subsequently, Carter had such an intention, nor were their deficits sufficient to encourage it. Johnson's move did, however, create a potential for application of the well known law of unintended consequences.

Regardless of his concern for inflation, Ford joined the traditional pattern of encouraging increases to Social Security. In his 1976 State of the Union address on 17 January, he proposed "catastrophic health insurance for everybody covered by Medicare. . . . I propose improving the Medicare and other health programs," he said, "to help those who really need more protection: older people and the poor." As for the basic Social Security program, his rhetoric could have come from Franklin Roosevelt or Lyndon Johnson. "Our Federal Social Security system for people who have worked hard and contributed to it all their lives is a vital part of our economic system. Its value is no longer debatable. In my budget for fiscal year 1977 I am recommending that the full cost of living increase in Social Security benefits be paid during the coming year."[51]

Ford, like all the presidents back to and including Roosevelt, described Social Security by implication as part of the American way of life, and suggested that it was an integral, and traditional, component of the American economic system—one that rewarded the thrift and hard work of individual Americans. Ford did break with tradition in injecting a cautionary note. "I am concerned," he said, "about the integrity of our Social Security trust fund that enables people—those retired and those still working who will retire—to count on this source of retirement income. Younger workers watch their deductions rise and wonder if they will be adequately protected in the future." He said that "we must meet this challenge head on," the challenge of a "Social Security trust fund [that] is headed for trouble. Unless we act soon to make sure the fund takes in as much as it pays out, there will be no security for old or young." He therefore recommended a tax increase on both employer and employee to take effect the following year.[52] The rhetoric had not changed. Ford used the same symbols that had justified increase and expansion to justify protection and preservation.

In his acceptance speech on 19 August 1976 following his nomination in Kansas City, Ford included Social Security, emphasizing both improvement and protection of the program. "We will ensure the integrity of the social security system," he said, "and improve Medicare so that our older citizens can enjoy the health and happiness that they have earned. There is no reason they should go broke just to get well."[53] Social Security and Medicare were therefore individual benefits earned by hard work—the American way. Those who have produced all their lives deserved a decent life as a reward and deserved to be protected from exploitation.

Ford's acceptance address reflected his acceptance of the essential pattern laid down by the New Deal and also of the rhetoric that the New Deal pattern had inspired. Social programs with their roots in the New Deal were nevertheless not his foremost consideration, or among his major concerns. In his final State of the Union speech,[54] he did not refer to Social Security among his list of accomplishments, nor did he include it in his recommendations to his successor, Jimmy Carter.

Although he was a Democrat, President Carter spoke less on Social Security than his predecessors. He did not stress the program in his acceptance speech, his inaugural address, or his State of the Union messages, although he did propose expanded health-care coverage. Social Security did not change notably during the Carter administration, except for revisions to the formula for indexing benefits to the cost of living, and the adoption in 1979 of a schedule of tax increases for many years to come. It is safe to assume that Carter did not include the program among his major emphases, but he did support social insurance, and when speaking of it, continued the traditional rhetoric.

As the election of 1980 neared, Carter emphasized Social Security more than he had previously, no doubt because of the long hostility of his opponent, Ronald Reagan, to the popular program. Carter emerged successful from a bitter campaign for renomination. In his acceptance address before the Democratic National Convention in New York on 14 August 1980 he referred to the "make-believe" world of the Republicans. "In their fantasy," he charged, "American, inner-city people and farm workers and laborers do not exist. Women, like children, are to be seen but not heard. The problems of working women are simply ignored. The elderly do not need Medicare." He accused the Republicans, now led by Reagan, of presenting proposals that were "an attack on everything that we've done in the achievement of social justice and decency that we've won in the last 50 years, ever since Franklin Delano Roosevelt's first term. They would make social security voluntary," he said.[55]

Ronald Reagan did not mention Social Security in his inaugural address, or in some early televised speeches, but he did reply to his critics in his first State of the Union message, on 18 February 1981. He said that he regretted fears that "unfounded stories have caused," fears that Social Security checks would be taken away from beneficiaries. "We will continue to fulfill the obligations that spring from our national conscience. Those who through no fault of their own must depend on the rest of us, the poverty-stricken, the disabled, the elderly, all those with true need can rest assured that the social safety net of programs they depend on are exempt from any cuts. The full retirement benefits of the more than 31 million Social Security recipients will be continued along with an annual cost of living increase. Medicare," he added, "will not be cut."[56]

The rhetoric sounded familiar. Reagan spoke of "obligations that spring from our national conscience," for example, but there were decided differences in tone from the language of earlier presidents. There was no mention of reward for work, or earned benefits. There was no hint that Social Security might be based upon American traditions. Instead, Reagan spoke of those who could not care for themselves and who needed help through no fault of their own. He spoke only of a needs-based program for the poor. Although he provided assurances, he carefully limited those assurances to current beneficiaries and made no mention of Social Security for future generations.

From Franklin D. Roosevelt through Jimmy Carter, presidential comments about Social Security showed a remarkable consistency, regardless of whether the president was conservative or liberal, Democrat or Republican, and regardless of the condition of the country. Reagan broke the pattern. His rhetoric in office questioned the foundation of Social Security, even though at the same time he sought to reassure those who depended upon the system.

Reagan's precandidate rhetoric had been overtly a frontal assault upon every principle of social insurance, yet the same rhetorical symbols that others had used in support also formed the basis of his attack. Social Security and related programs, he had argued, were incompatible with individualism, the prime symbol of American political discourse. They threatened American liberty by discarding the country's tradition of limited government.

Rarely are the effects of the spoken word and the written word the same. Franklin Roosevelt was a master speaker, and his written words retain their force. John Kennedy similarly excelled in both media. In Lyndon Johnson's case, his words in writing often are powerful, usually more powerful than when he spoke them. In Reagan's case, the effects are sharply different. On paper, Reagan's rhetoric is flat and uninspiring. As a speaker delivering a prepared text, he was unexcelled. His powerful rhetoric developed an undercurrent of support throughout the country at the same time that his ideas were ridiculed. His delivery on the AMA's recording for "Operation Coffeecup" has to be heard to experience its intensity and effectiveness. His masterful performance for Goldwater in 1964 was owing entirely to the sound of his words, not their content. The content was a typical presentation of "The Speech," which moved millions when spoken but affected only the True Believer when in print.

All presidents since FDR have had some effect upon Social Security. The rhetoric that Roosevelt inspired implemented the program and continued to justify protecting and expanding it. Only Reagan differed. He often adopted the rhetoric of his predecessors but used it skillfully to reverse its previous effect: to question, to undermine, and to suggest alternatives.

8

The Special Problem
of Health Care

The Fortunes to Be Made

If we are to understand why Medicare has special problems—although they are less serious than the critics allege, they nevertheless are real—it is necessary to understand the problems of the American health care delivery system in general. The health care system in the United States involves certain irrationalities that are peculiar to itself. In general, it evolved to incorporate two primary factors. First, practitioners—generally physicians and dentists—provided services and collected a fee for each specific service. Second, hospitals—where physicians provided care for serious illness—emerged as predominantly nonprofit institutions, most likely under the sponsorship of public, religious, or philanthropic organizations. Nursing homes tended to be an exception to the nonprofit rule; generally, they always have been proprietary institutions.

Medical economics has dealt a blow to each of these factors. Fee-for-service medicine has proven to be too expensive to dominate in a modern competitive marketplace. Moreover, it tends to ignore wellness; that is, rather than promoting healthy lifestyles and preventive care, it concentrates on curing pathologies after they develop. With a fee charged for each service, there are economic incentives to require numerous procedures and to order a maximum number of diagnostic tests. Economic factors similarly encourage the selection of the most expensive procedure when several are available.

For decades, there have been fortunes to be made by investing in nursing homes. In recent years hospitals have come to present the same dynamics. In a too-little-noticed development, nonprofit hospitals have almost completely lost out in the marketplace to proprietary—that is, profit-making—institutions. The few nonprofit hospitals remaining often behave the same as those run for profit.

Just as specialization has come to dominate American medicine, so has specialization affected hospitals, as institutions emphasize profitable services and eliminate those that nonprofit hospitals once operated as a community service. So profitable have hospitals become that they compete vigorously for patients—and investors. Nonprofit institutions in general, and teaching hospitals in particular, are an endangered species.

Fee-for-service private medicine plus burgeoning technology began at least by the 1930s to force the costs of medical care to rise considerably faster than the general cost of living. Blue Cross plans emerged to provide the insurance principle as protection against rising costs of hospitalization. Adopting the principle of community rating, Blue Cross guaranteed hospital care as needed for those who paid a monthly fee. The fee was equal for every member in a given region. Thus, those who were elderly or in ill health could be protected for the same cost as those who were young and healthy.

In the absence of regulation, such a situation could not continue in the American economy. Private insurance companies recognized the huge profit to be made in offering coverage to young, healthy persons at rates below those of Blue Cross— they were able to keep their expenditures low by refusing to issue policies to anyone presenting higher risk. As private companies persuaded those presenting the lowest risk to switch from Blue Cross to their own policies, Blue Cross plans were left increasingly with high-risk—therefore high-cost—members. In order to survive in any form, Blue Cross had no alternative but to abandon the community rating that shared risk among all and to adopt the practices of the insurance companies. Thus the unregulated market succeeded in destroying Blue Cross as it originally existed: as a plan to provide coverage for the entire community at a reasonable cost for all.

The Blue Cross experiment had failed. The result was a Blue Cross that was little different from the companies that had attacked it. American health care came increasingly to be provided through insurance companies that offer coverage at reasonable rates to those who need it least and offer no coverage at all or coverage that is prohibitively expensive to everyone else. Because of the ability of large groups to negotiate lower rates, numerous employers came to offer health-insurance coverage as a fringe benefit to their employees. Health insurance as a fringe benefit of employment came ultimately to be the only possibility of coverage for most Americans.

The resulting dynamic not only resulted in increasing numbers of people with no coverage—individual policies became too expensive for nearly everyone, and small employers rarely would provide insurance for their employees—but in forcing the costs of health care to rise at an even more rapid rate. There came to be no connection between cost and the patient. Insurance paid everything that was paid. The insured patient generally had no concern for the size of his or her bills, because "insurance covered it." The many without insurance often obtained no care or received care in hospital emergency rooms which by law could not turn them away. Emergency room care is the most expensive care possible. When such patients could pay no more, or could pay nothing, hospitals had to find payment somewhere. They therefore increased their other charges to compensate, thus raising health costs and insurance premiums still higher.

Competition among hospitals has reflected a similar dynamic. To compete, hospitals have sought to obtain every piece of equipment, necessary or not. If a community has, for example, four hospitals but has needed only one enormously expensive piece of equipment such as an MRI or a CAT scan, each hospital nevertheless has felt the need to have one for competitive reasons. As the trend has accelerated, some hospitals have sought to have multiple pieces of equipment for extra convenience. As a matter of fact, the community with four hospitals probably has more hospitals than it needs. Communities now are very often—if not generally—overbuilt because of competition among companies seeking profit. When there are too many hospitals, there are too many beds unoccupied and the cost per bed rises sharply.

This is the situation that America, virtually alone in the world, has developed. A system has emerged that provides nearly all health care through profitmaking institutions and caregivers, and one that finances most of that profit through another profitmaking institution, the insurance company. Such companies are notoriously inefficient. Long ago, for example, it was reported that Massachusetts Blue Cross, one company in one limited jurisdiction, employed more clerks than the entire health delivery system in Canada. America's health care costs far more for each citizen than health care anywhere else in the world, at the same time that America has a higher proportion of its citizens with no coverage than is the case in any other industrialized country.

To those who argue that America cannot afford to do more for its citizens, it should be pointed out that doing more—if done correctly—should cost less. Americans already pay for health coverage in ways that more often than not are hidden. Automobile executives, for example, some years ago remarked that they spent more for health coverage for their employees than for steel. That, of course, drives up the costs of automobiles. The large amount added to the cost of an automobile is only one of the more dramatic examples. It is far from the only one, or the most costly one.

This was the situation that encouraged President Clinton on 20 November 1993 to propose his plan for providing health care coverage to the entire population. Rejecting the single-payer plan as politically infeasible, the Clinton plan would have provided health coverage for most of the population through regional alliances. States would have established the alliances, which would have contracted with several plans to produce a comprehensive benefit package. Thus, the proposal would have retained the elements of the traditional system, private practice of medicine and coverage through insurance companies. It also would have permitted citizens to choose among several options, because each alliance would have had varied programs, including managed-care plans and those offering coverage based on traditional fee-for-service to health care providers.

Financing for the Clinton plan would have come from several sources. Employers would have been required to offer health coverage to their employees, paying 80 percent of the cost of a basic plan. There was to have been a cap on the amount an employer would have been required to pay: no more than 7.9 percent of payroll, and less for small firms. Employees would have chosen from among the options offered by the alliance in their region and would have paid 20 percent of the cost of an average plan, the percentage varying if the option chosen cost more or less than the average. Employees with family income of less than $40,000 per year were to pay less.

There were to have been federal subsidies based on income to permit unemployed citizens to purchase care from the region's alliance. If combined employer/employee payments were insufficient to pay for a plan (as might have been the case, for example, when the coverage was for low-income workers), federal subsidies would cover the shortfall. Large employers, those with 5,000 employees or more, would have been able to form their own "corporate alliances," as could some union plans.

The Clinton plan would have eliminated much of Medicaid. Instead of care through Medicaid, indigent patients would have received coverage through the alliances, paid for by state and federal funds. At least initially, Medicare would have remained without change, except to add a new benefit: prescription drug coverage for outpatient care. The plan called for new grants to states to cover long-term services to the disabled.

The Clinton plan sought to control costs by limiting the amount that insurance premium rates could increase. They would have been restricted to increases no greater than increases in the gross domestic product (GDP). Financing for the new prescription drug coverage, for long-term care benefits, and for the premium subsidies would have come from limits on premium costs, reductions in the growth of Medicare and Medicaid spending, an increased tobacco tax, and a payroll tax on corporate alliances.

There was additional flexibility also. States could have opted out of the system in order to provide their own plans for universal coverage, including single-payer plans. The plan provided for the proposed system to come into effect on a state-by-state basis, as each state set up its alliances, as early as 1996, and no later than 1998.[1]

The plan had many virtues. It avoided radical approaches that nearly always—especially to Americans—are frightening. It would have been consistent with previous practices, taking care to avoid upsetting the fundamental elements of America's health care delivery system. It would have provided virtually universal coverage, and it had some cost-containment provisions.

It also had many weaknesses, some of which were the same as its virtues. In avoiding radical approaches, it retained the worst elements of America's health delivery system. Alliances and managed care, to be sure, would have increased efficiency and reduced some costs. Retention of insurance companies as the primary payment mechanisms, on the other hand, meant retention of gross inefficiencies. Similarly, the system had to generate profits to operate, profits not only to health care providers, but also to insurance companies and investors.

At first, even opponents of the Clinton plan assumed that something would pass and that the most they could do would be to modify it so that it would be less to their disliking. After all, the public feared loss of coverage, and there was strong pressure to reform the system. Ultimately, however, the support fell apart because of a combination of factors. Special interest lobbies spent almost unlimited funds to defeat the plan. They portrayed it as a government takeover of the health care system, something that it clearly was not, and something that the Clinton administration had worked strenuously and successfully to keep it from being. As a matter of fact, the proposal would have been stronger had there been *greater* government involvement and *more* government control.

Small business groups immediately protested the requirement that they provide coverage. Pizza chains, for example, companies that offered coverage to their employees in other countries because of government mandates, argued that they could not survive if they had to offer the same benefits in the United States. Never mind that they thrive in foreign environments that place more restrictions upon them than the United States does; never mind that they thrive where they must offer health coverage and other benefits lacking here. Herman Cain, the CEO of Godfather's Pizza, went on television complaining that the cost of pizzas would increase if Godfather's had to give benefits to its employees. When offered the choice of denying health coverage to millions of Americans, or paying twenty-five cents more for a pizza, Mr. Cain assumed that Americans would make the correct choice: deny the coverage. If the outcome of the Clinton effort is any indication, Mr. Cain was correct, at least for a time.

Opponents of the plan also argued against limits on premiums. Such limits, they protested, would prevent competition! Moreover, they would lead to rationing of services that companies could no longer afford to provide. Opponents also appealed to the elderly, saying that reliance on savings from Medicare to finance the program would threaten the system and that the Clinton plan would have the effect of forcing everyone into HMOs.

This enormous and unprecedented effort by special interests, combined with inexperience and an unwillingness to compromise on the part of the Clinton administration, brought all momentum to a halt. Washington rarely, if ever, works without flexibility and compromise. The Clinton plan, assumed at first by supporters and opponents alike to be inevitable in one form or another, did not receive a negative vote in Congress—it did not ever even make it to a vote. It truly died, with no bang but a whimper.

Journalists Haynes Johnson and David Broder have written a remarkable study of the failure of the Clinton plan and what it reflects of American politics and society, *The System: The American Way of Politics at the Breaking Point*.[2] Their book is based on careful observation and on interviews with all the major figures who participated in the effort. It amply documents the errors of the Clinton administration and the pervasive effect of the vast sums of money that numerous interests successfully devoted to defeating the plan—and to dominating American public policy.

The defeat of the Clinton plan contributed to a startling turnaround in Congress. The 1994 elections brought Republican control to both the House of Representatives and the Senate. Republicans had not controlled the full Congress for four decades. The new majority tended to consider defeat of the universal plan to be a victory. Rather than proposing their own plan for increased coverage, they turned their attention to the high costs of Medicare and sought to place tight restrictions on the program's growth. The Democrats described the restrictions as "cuts," and this description outraged the Republicans. They retorted that they proposed to *increase* spending, but at a slower rate.

The Republicans were correct, but so were the Democrats. The rate of increase that the Republicans favored would have led to marked reductions in benefits as costs and the population covered increased. The Republican plan passed in Congress, but President Clinton vetoed it. He charged that the Republicans, who also included a tax reduction in the legislation, were seeking to take benefits away from Medicare patients in order to finance tax cuts for the wealthy. The president won the public relations battle, and the Republican plan died.

Johnson and Broder saw both the Republican actions in opposition to the Clinton plan and the Democratic response to the Republicans' efforts as obstructionist. Something, they argued, had to be done about Medicare. As they described it, "President Clinton was right in 1993 and 1994 in saying that runaway health costs were robbing America of its future. Republicans foiled his solution. Now, it appeared he was going to try to foil theirs. It was exactly the kind of behavior that was destroying public faith in The System."[3]

As Johnson and Broder put it, there was "hardball" when necessary, as the American Association of Retired Persons (AARP) discovered. Politicians often fear, or profess to fear, the AARP because of the organization's huge membership. That membership, however, is far from monolithic, and one would be hard pressed to demonstrate that it is predominantly political. Johnson and Broder demonstrated that, however fearsome it may be, AARP can be defanged. Its lobbyist, John Rother, described a "two-pronged approach" that the Republican antagonists to the president adopted with regard to AARP.

To head off any likelihood of massive AARP opposition to their Medicare proposals, Speaker of the House Newt "Gingrich and his allies communicated the message that 'we know we have to talk to you. We understand that you guys have power to torpedo this, and we don't want that.'" Senator Alan Simpson (R–Wyoming) at the same time was the "enforcer" for the Republicans as they "flexed their muscle." He announced plans for senatorial hearings on AARP's finances and on its tax-exempt status. Just before the hearings were to be held, the senator "paid a call to the AARP board and said, 'I want you to know that the intensity of my investigation of AARP will vary directly with the intensity of your efforts to fight the Medicare changes.' Rother insisted that AARP was not intimidated, but it waited until very late in the fall to announce its opposition to the Republican plan."[4]

Johnson and Broder have harsh words for many players in today's system.

> The story of the life and death of health reform shines a harsh light on the way The System—and the men and women in it— succeeds or fails. As Paul Starr, the Princeton scholar and author who played a major part in designing the Clinton health care re- form, ruefully said later, "the collapse of health care reform in the first two years of the Clinton administration will go down as one of the great lost political opportunities in American his- tory. It is a story of compromises that never happened, of deals that were never closed, of Republicans, moderate Democrats, and key interest groups that backpedaled from proposals they themselves had earlier co-sponsored or endorsed. It is also a story of strategic miscalculations on the part of the President and those of us who advised him." He also accurately said, "The Republicans enjoyed a double triumph, killing reform and then watching jurors find the President guilty. It was the political equivalent of the perfect crime."[5]

David Gergen is a Republican who served in the Clinton White House and therefore is able to provide an unusual per- spective. Writing in *U.S. News and World Report* he noted that even Johnson and Broder, who followed the health care plan's defeat as closely as anyone, seemed "startled by the power and skill of the most influential players on the field: national lobbyists."[6]

Gergen pointed out that, after having been snubbed in their efforts to compromise, the Health Insurance Association of

America and the National Federation of Independent Business mobilized against the plan, and along with other groups spent "at least $100 million (and perhaps three times that), greatly exceeding the combined amount all candidates spent running for president of the United States in 1992, a year that marked a record for campaign spending." He, Johnson, and Broder agree that the lobbies have become "crypto-political parties of their own—unelected and unaccountable." It is important, Gergen noted, that we begin paying closer attention to them.[7]

Some observers, such as Newt Gingrich, saw the failure of health care reform as evidence that the system worked. Arguing that inaction was the best outcome, they pointed to changes occurring in the marketplace. Not all observers were so sanguine. Even Bill Gradison of the Health Insurance Association of America, an association that opposed the Clinton plan most fervently, remarked a year after the plan's defeat that one could argue that government's failure gave the private market "a chance to develop without major hurdles. On the other hand," he said, "there are actions which only the government can take which are really needed." For example, he added, "I told my members when Congress went home in 1994 that there were no winners and a lot of losers in the great health care debate. The problems were still there. The number of uninsured was already at unacceptable levels and was going to rise. The level of health care inflation, while moderating, was still too high. These things require action. That is still my view." As Johnson and Broder mentioned, it was their view as well.[8]

Many of the developments that critics charged would emerge if the Clinton plan were adopted are now changing the face of American medical practice—without that plan. Potentially, HMOs can provide superb care, and many do. The primary emphasis in managed care, on the other hand, is on suppressing costs rather than benefiting the patient. Managed care is coming now to dominate the health care industry. The charges that the Clinton plan would have effected a "government takeover of medicine" were so inaccurate as to have been absurd. The charge that it would have eliminated patient choice was hardly less so. That plan would have preserved a private fee-for-service option, which Americans traditionally equate with freedom of choice.

The rush in the industry toward managed care, on the other hand, is truly destroying the rather limited freedom of choice that previously existed. It probably is too early to judge accurately the overall effects on quality of care, but the anecdotal evidence accumulates that emphasizing the bottom line can work to deprive patients of needed, sometimes essential, treatment. Congressional hostility toward trial lawyers and punitive damages has even made it impossible in most instances for patients, however mistreated, to bring suit against their HMOs.

This is the situation facing the country at the same time that it is becoming fearful that Medicare cannot survive as currently constituted. The situation is one of medical economics. Medicare pays the full cost for a wide range of health services. To be sure, managed care recently has caused a slowing in cost increases. Traditionally, though, the cost of health services has escalated rapidly, and it appears as if the cost is poised to increase once more as the techniques of managed care reach their limits.

Certainly much of the perceived "crisis" reflects considerations more political than economic. This is especially true in view of the budget surplus. Furthermore, the heavily publicized predictions in 1995 and 1996 that Medicare would go bankrupt in seven years or so are merely a link in a long chain of such predictions spreading back for decades—predictions each time that the system had only seven years left. It was political campaigning, not primarily economics, that brought them to the public's attention, campaigning in which opponents of Medicare and social insurance in general skillfully used the predictions to justify their assaults on the program.

It is worth noting that the 1998 report of the trustees continues to predict trouble for Medicare—seven years in the future!

Nevertheless, although the situation is not one of "crisis," there clearly are reasons for concern. Without doubt, some things must change. Currently the discussion centers solely on Medicare itself: In order to be saved, it must be "reformed." By the terms of this debate, "reform" can come in only one of three ways: large amounts of additional revenues must be provided to pay for the system's benefits, those benefits must be reduced, or additional numbers of people must be denied coverage.

Providing a huge infusion of additional revenues—despite America's huge wealth—seems not to be feasible. Those revenues would have to come from additional taxes or from general revenues. The critics argue that providing them from general revenues would make it impossible to keep the budget in balance without substantial tax increases. It is interesting that the sudden and unanticipated achievement of budget surpluses now possibly suggests otherwise. In any case, the political climate demands budget balance and seems to forbid general tax increases. Increasing taxes specifically for Medicare also seems out of the question. Increasing fees for recipients similarly is politically charged and would affect most severely those least able to pay.

Thus, those who charged the Democrats with practicing demagoguery on the Medicare issue felt justified in their charges. If tax increases are out of the question and fees cannot be increased, then Medicare could not continue as constituted without reducing benefits—unless it were to become means tested. Means testing also is obviously another way of reducing benefits. Less obviously, it is a means of destroying the program: it would require millions of taxpayers to fund a system that would limit its benefits to others.

The only true solution is to look at the American health care delivery system as a whole. Other industrial countries provide comprehensive health care for all their citizens. America is wealthier than they, yet we have become convinced that it is too expensive to do as they do. We already spend *more* than those countries. Surely we could provide their benefits with what we already spend. In any case, it is nonsense to say that among the world's advanced industrial countries, only the wealthiest, America, has too few resources to care for its entire population.

President Clinton in his 1998 State of the Union address proposed devoting a portion of the budget surplus to Medicare. This would be wise; it would undoubtedly keep the system going until it is politically possible to find a larger solution. What we do *not* need is a "reform" that would increase the number of Americans who have no health coverage. To provide the coverage that other countries provide—and provide it at lower costs—requires more than "saving" Medicare, more than "reforming" it. Ultimately, to save Medicare requires that we also reform, if not "save," America's general system of delivering health care. One proposal with considerable promise is for the federal government to mandate—and support—comprehensive state systems of universal coverage.

Whether the larger solution can be accomplished conservatively, as the Clinton administration attempted to do, or whether it requires adopting a single-payer system—state systems, a federal system, a combination, or some other approach—is certainly not yet clear. What is clear is that reform must eliminate as much inefficiency as possible (for example, by eliminating the need for clerks in physicians' offices to master hundreds of different procedures to secure reimbursement from insurance companies); must restructure the fee system that rewards certain specialists inordinately as compared with internists, pediatricians, and others who provide general care; must discover ways to provide comprehensive coverage of high quality to the entire population without resorting to emergency rooms as substitutes for general health deliverers; must reduce the current hemorrhaging of funds from the system into exorbitant profits; and must restore the original Blue Cross principle of community rating in order to keep costs reasonable on a per capita basis.

In all probability, it will be necessary to restructure the delivery system by emphasizing the nurse practitioner as the primary care provider. As to concerns for quality, nurse practitioners are well educated professionals who recognize their limitations, and who—within the limits of their practice—as a rule have considerably more hands-on patient experience than physicians. They can provide care of high quality and at much less cost than most physicians. HMOs, managed-care plans, and individual physicians whose practices extend over broad geographic areas that limit their availability already utilize nurse practitioners extensively. The result has been highly favorable, with nurse practitioners frequently becoming patients' primary practitioners of choice.

The point is that the critics are correct in some of their concerns. Many of the concerns are based on genuine conditions that do require change. Medicare, however, is only the most obvious part of the picture. American medicine is already undergoing changes and must be changed further. Medicare is part of the broader pattern of American medicine, and it is best not to consider it in a vacuum. More important than "saving" Medicare is reform of the entire American system of health care delivery.

Changes are indeed occurring, but whether those changes are leading to reform is questionable. We must put aside our political differences and respond to reality, not ideology. A great opportunity passed in 1993. If the society does not engineer another such opportunity—and reasonably quickly—reform will become progressively more difficult.

There is hardly any question that reform will come one way or another. The question is whether reform will come before the situation truly does become one of crisis. If so, that reform could produce an outcome generated by reasoned and nonideological planning and compromise that can avoid mass misery. The alternative is to follow the traditional pattern of delay until a true crisis results that damages much of the population. Then, the response is likely to be hasty and perhaps unwise action in response to a panic.

It would be well to anticipate the crisis and avert it by reforming medical practice, not merely by attempting to reform Medicare. That would be the rational approach, and probably the easier approach if we have the skillful political leadership required to counter those who believe that government has no role to play in bettering the lives of Americans. To those who would argue that this would be the most "un-American" approach, let it be said that this was precisely the approach that brought us Social Security, the most successful income maintenance program in history. The American people, working together, have accomplished great reforms before when needed—they can do it again.

In the meantime, the immediate challenge before us is not to make major reforms, it is simply to preserve the most successful income maintenance program in history. To that challenge my final chapter returns.

9

Some Final Words

In some matters, the public appears to be throwing off media domination and the efforts of manipulators. Witness, for example, the frenzy within the beltway regarding the President's sex life and the refusal outside the beltway to be concerned. The public is similarly resisting the more extreme arguments of Social Security's enemies. The following items of information should be sufficient for informed judgment regarding the less extreme, but no less serious, proposals for reform:

- The intermediate projections of the trustees are based on pessimistic assumptions that the economy will fare far worse than it has for many years. Their optimistic projections are more realistic. Regardless of the propaganda, there will be a higher proportion of the population in the work force in 2030 than there was in 1965. Pressure from the baby boomers will be partially offset by reduction in the number of younger beneficiaries, and in any case, the boomers ultimately will pass from the scene. The average life span has increased since Social Security began paying benefits, but not as dramatically as the propaganda would have it. The average remaining life expectancy for a woman at age 65 is fewer than five years longer in the 1990s than it was in 1940; for a man it is fewer than three years longer.

- Money in the trust funds is invested in government securities, which pay interest back into the funds. The government has not misappropriated the money. Government bonds do represent value, just as currency does.
- The calculations of those who popularize the idea of privatization are distorted to favor their point of view. Even when their math is accurate, their assumptions are not. They ignore the loss of disability and survivors' benefits—which represent some $514,000 in protection—and of Medicare. They select a single worker as the example so that they can ignore benefits for a spouse. They also select a highly paid worker, whose benefits are proportionally less than for those of lower pay. Moreover, they ignore Social Security's inflation protection, and above all, they deny economic reality—that in a privatized system, some people will lose their money. A rising stock market, even if it rises forever, does not mean that all stocks rise in value. In Great Britain, huge numbers of citizens who opted into a privatized system have been shattered financially. That experience has received little publicity in the United States, but it obviously should suggest extreme caution before substituting any degree of privatization for any part of the existing Social Security system. A security salesman who promises what "privatizers" do would be prosecuted. Social Security's record is established. It has never failed to provide its checks when due. Private industry cannot truthfully make the same claim.
- All objective studies conclude that Social Security represents an excellent value to the worker for the money paid in and will continue to do so.
- Means testing Social Security would change its nature and destroy the system. Universal coverage regardless of need is a major strong point of the system.

Millionaires do receive Social Security, but they also pay into it. Their benefits represent a smaller return on what they pay in than do the benefits of lower paid workers.

- Social Security bears no relation to a Ponzi scheme (or pyramid scheme). Allegations that it does reflect either ignorance or attempts to mislead. An example of the latter is Milton Friedman's op-ed piece in the *New York Times*.[1] He said of Social Security that what supporters call a compact between generations, "opponents call a Ponzi scheme." Now, as a Nobel Laureate in economics, Friedman surely knows what a Ponzi scheme is and what it is not. His duplicitous phrasing did not actually call Social Security a Ponzi scheme—he doubtless knows better—but was calculated to leave that impression. Ponzi schemes are unsustainable because they require a geometric progression. With Social Security each generation pays benefits to its dependent population. These payments are sustainable indefinitely—in fact, in one form or another, every generation throughout history has supported its dependents.
- Social Security operates at a level of administrative efficiency that is far higher than that of any private program, which is to say that it operates at a far lower cost, putting more of its resources into benefits than any private program can manage.
- The idea of "intergenerational inequities" as applied to Social Security is a fraudulent notion designed as political propaganda, not economics or ethics. Social Security provides protection to all age groups and to all economic classes.

All projections over any great length of time are questionable. Using long-term projections as the basis for making radical changes in a vital program that has served the country well and is continuing to do so would be the height of folly. Changes of course may be required from time to time, but the sound, conservative, and wise approach is to make them carefully and incrementally.

Make any necessary changes based upon sound advice from disinterested parties. Reject the pleas from those who have ideological points to score or who have fortunes to be made.

Make no mistake about it. Virtually all of the information inundating the country today about Social Security originates from those sources only—those who have ideological points to score, and those who have fortunes to be made.

Appendix

Text of Recording for "Operation Coffeecup" (discussed on pages 61–63)

I. Ronald Reagan Speaks Out Against Socialized Medicine

My name is Ronald Reagan. I have been asked to talk on the several subjects that have to do with the problems of the day. It must seem presumptuous to some of you that a member of my profession would stand here and attempt to talk to anyone on serious problems that face the nation and the world. It would be strange if it were otherwise.

Most of us in Hollywood are very well aware of the concept or the misconception that many people, our fellow citizens, have about people in show business. It was only a generation ago that people of my profession couldn't be buried in the churchyard. Of course, the world has improved since then. We can be buried now. As a matter of fact, the eagerness of some of you to perform that service gets a little frightening at times.

Now back in 1927 an American socialist, Norman Thomas, six times candidate for president on the Socialist Party ticket, said the American people would never vote for socialism. But he said under the name of liberalism the American people would adopt every fragment of the socialist program.

There are many ways in which our government has invaded the precincts of private citizens, the method of earning a living. Our government is in business to the extent of owning more than 19,000 businesses covering 47 different lines of activity. This amounts to a fifth of the total industrial capacity of the United States.

But at the moment I'd like to talk about another way because this threat is with us and at the moment is more imminent. One of the traditional methods of imposing statism or socialism on people has been by way of medicine. It's very easy to disguise a medical program as a humanitarian project. Most people are a little reluctant to oppose anything that suggests medical care for people who possibly can't afford it. Now, the American people, if you put it to them about socialized medicine and gave them a chance to choose, would unhesitatingly vote against it. We have an example of this. Under the Truman administration it was proposed that we have a compulsory health insurance program for all people in the United States, and, of course, the American people unhesitatingly rejected this.

So, with the American people on record as not wanting socialized medicine, Congressman Forand introduced the Forand Bill. This was the idea that all people of social security age should be brought under a program of compulsory health insurance. Now, this would not only be our senior citizens, this would be the dependents and those who are disabled, this would be young people if they are dependents of someone eligible for social security. Now, Congressman Forand brought the program out on that idea for that particular group of people. But Congressman Forand was subscribing to this foot-in-the-door philosophy because he said, "If we can only break through and get our foot inside the door, then we can expand the program after that." Walter Reuther said, "It's no secret that the United Automobile Workers are officially on record as backing a program of national health insurance." And by national health insurance he meant socialized medicine for every American.

Well, let's see what the socialists themselves had to say about it. They say, "Once the Forand Bill is passed this nation will be provided with a mechanism for socialized medicine capable of indefinite expansion in every direction until it includes the entire population." Well, we can't say we haven't been warned. Now Congressman Forand is no longer a congressman of the United States Government. He has been replaced, not in his particular assignment, but in his backing of such a bill, by Congressman King of California. It is presented in the idea of a great emergency that millions of our senior citizens are unable to provide needed medical care. But this ignores the fact that in the last decade 127 million of our citizens, in just ten years, have come under the protection of some form of privately owned medical or hospital insurance.

Now, the advocates of this bill, when you try to oppose it, challenge you on an emotional basis. They say, "What would you do, throw these poor old people out to die with no medical attention?" That's ridiculous and of course no one has advocated it. As a matter of fact, in the last session of Congress a bill was adopted known as the Kerr-Mills Bill. Now, without even allowing this bill to be tried to see if it works, they have introduced this King Bill which is really the Forand Bill. What is the Kerr-Mills Bill? It is a frank recognition of the medical need or problem of our senior citizens that I have mentioned. And it is provided from the Federal Government money to the states and the local communities that can be used at the discretion of the state to help those people who need it. Now what reason could the other people have for backing a bill which says we insist on compulsory health insurance for senior citizens on a basis of age alone regardless of whether they are worth millions of dollars, whether they have an income, whether they're protected by their own insurance, whether they have savings. I think we could be excused for believing that, as ex-Congressman Forand said, this was simply an excuse to bring about what they wanted all the time: Socialized medicine. James Madison, in 1788, speaking to the Virginia Convention, said: "Since the general civilization of mankind I believe there are more instances of the abridgment of the freedom of the people by gradual and silent encroachment of those in power than by violent and sudden usurpations."

They want to attach this bill to social security and they say, "Here is a great insurance program, now instituted, now working." Let's take a look at social security itself. Again, very few of us disagree with the original premise that there should be some form of saving that would keep destitution from following unemployment by reason of death, disability, or old age. And to this end social security was adopted. But it was never intended to supplant private saving, private insurance, pension programs of unions and industries. Now, in our country under our free enterprise system we have seen medicine reach the greatest heights that it has in any country in the world. Today the relationship between patient and doctor in this country is something to be envied any place. The privacy, the care that is given to a person, the right to choose a doctor, the right to go from one doctor to the other. But let's also look from the other side at the freedom the doctor loses. A doctor would be reluctant to say this. Well, like you. I'm only a patient so I can say it in his behalf. The doctor begins to lose freedom. It's like telling a lie and one leads to another. First you decide that the doctor can have so many patients. They are equally divided among the various doctors by the government. But then doctors were equally divided geographically. So a doctor decides he wants to practice in one town and the government has to say to him, You can't live in that town. They already have enough doctors. You have to go someplace else. And from here it's only a short step to dictating where he will go. This is a freedom that I wonder whether any of us have the right to take from any human being. I know how I'd feel if you, my fellow citizens, decided that to be an actor I had to become a government employee and work in a national theater. Take it into your own occupation or that of your husband. All of us can see what happens once you establish the precedent that the government can determine a man's working place and his work methods, determine his employment. From here it's a short step to all the rest of socialism to determining his pay. And pretty soon your son won't decide when he's in school, where he will go or what he will do for a living. He will wait for the government to tell him where he will go to work and what he will do.

In this country of ours took place the greatest revolution that has ever taken place in world's history, the only true revolution. Every other revolution simply exchanged one set of rulers for another. But here for the first time in all the thousands of years in man's relation to man a little group of men, the Founding Fathers, for the first time established the idea that you and I had within ourselves the God-given right and ability to determine our own destiny. This freedom was built into our government with safeguards. We talk democracy today and, strangely, we let democracy begin to assume the aspect of majority rule is all that is needed. Well, majority rule is a fine aspect of democracy, provided there are guarantees written into our government concerning the rights of the individual and of the minorities. What can we do about this? Well, you and I can do a great deal. We can write to our congressmen and to our senators. We can say right now that we want no further encroachment on these individual liberties and freedoms. And at the moment the key issue is: We do not want socialized medicine. Now, you may think when I say write to the congressman or the senator that this is like writing fan mail to a television program. It isn't. In Washington today 40,000 letters, less than 100 per congressman, are evidence of a trend in public thinking. Representative Halleck of Indiana has said, "When the American people want something from Congress, regardless of its political complexion, if they make their wants known, Congress does what the people want." So write. It's as simple as finding just the name of your congressman or your senator, and then you address your letter to that individual's name. If he's a congressman to the House Office Building, Washington, D.C.; if he's a senator to the Senate Office Building, Washington, D.C. And if this man writes back to you and tells you that he, too, is for free enterprise, but we have these great services, and so forth that must be performed by government, don't let him get away with it. Show that you have not been convinced. Write a letter right back and tell him that you believe in government economy and fiscal responsibility, that you know that governments don't tax to get

the money they need, governments will always find a need for
the money they get, and that you demand the continuation of
our traditional free enterprise system. You and I can do this. The
only way we can do it is by writing to our congressman even if
we believe that he's on our side to begin with. Write to
strengthen his hand. Give him the ability to stand before his
colleagues in Congress and say, I heard from my constituents
and this is what they want. If you don't, this program, I promise
you, will pass just as surely as the sun will come up tomorrow.
And behind it will come other Federal programs that will invade
every area of freedom as we have known it in this country. Until
one day, as Norman Thomas said, we will awake to find that we
have socialism. And if you don't do this and if I don't do it, one
of these days you and I are going to spend our sunset years
telling our children and our children's children what it once was
like in America when men were free.

II. Socialized Medicine and You

[Male voice, unidentified]

Mr. Reagan's concern is very real. And all of us who are
equally concerned should follow his advice. Now you may wonder just what sort of letter to write your congressman. The answer is almost any letter, so long as it reflects your thinking,
your convictions, your feelings. And so long as you use your
own words, and put them in your own handwriting.

Perhaps a little background on the subject of socialized medicine will prove helpful to you. To begin with, socialized medicine simply means compulsory national health insurance, medicine controlled and administered by the federal government,
financed through compulsory taxation. For many years, an attempt has been made to socialize the practice of medicine
through the Social Security tax mechanism. The American people, and Congress, have rejected overwhelmingly these attempts.

Last year, Representative Forand attempted to establish the principle of socialized medicine by applying it only to the elderly—at first. He, and others like him, counted on the concern we all feel for those of the aged in need of help. The Forand Bill failed. But this year, another congressman has stepped forward to lead the forces of socialized medicine: Representative King, of California. It is his measure, H.R. 4222, or the King Bill, that now threatens the free practice of medicine.

The supporters of the King Bill contend that most of the aged are in poor health and that most of the aged are financially unable to pay for their own medical care. The fact is that most of the aged are in reasonably good health. And most are in reasonably good shape financially. Surveys prove both points.

However, I'm sure that we all recognize that some of our older people are in poor health and some can't afford to pay for the health care they need. That's why the doctors of America strongly supported the legislation passed during the last Congress: the so-called Kerr-Mills Law. They felt, and have always felt, that people who need medical help should get it, but that tax dollars should not be used to pay the medical and hospital bills of those who are perfectly able to pay their own.

Physicians favored the Kerr-Mills Law because it would help those of the elderly who need help, help them quickly, and effectively, and do so without wasting either the taxpayer's money or destroying the basic American freedoms involved in our system of medical practice. The Kerr-Mills Law is now being put into effect. It permits the individual states to guarantee to every American over sixty-five who needs help the health care he requires. It benefits all older persons unable to meet the cost of a serious or chronic illness. It specifically allows the individual states to run their own programs. It provides for local administration and local determination of need, and is financed from both the federal and state general tax funds.

Without even giving this program a chance to prove what it could do, the King Bill, H.R. 4222, was introduced. Here's how it would work. The federal government would buy a limited amount of hospitalization, nursing-home care, home-health services, and outpatient hospital diagnostic services for all eligible to receive Social Security retirement payments, regardless of their financial needs. The number of days the beneficiary could receive these services is limited. And the patient would be required to pay ten dollars a day for the first nine days spent in a hospital, and twenty dollars for each complete diagnostic study made. Physicians' services in the fields of radiology, pathology, physiatry, and anesthesiology would be included, plus the services of interns and residents and those serving the outpatient clinics.

There is little doubt but what the program would soon be expanded to include all physicians' services, as well as to cover the entire population, thus completely socializing medicine in the United States. The federal government would set up the rules and regulations under which the program would operate. And every one who pays Social Security taxes would help pay the bill, because taxes would be raised beyond the nine percent of taxable payroll already scheduled in the years ahead.

I'm sure many of you are wondering why there's any objection to using the Social Security system to finance medical care for the aged. Well first of all, it is a misnomer to think of Social Security as being insurance. In the *Nestor* v. *Fleming* case heard before the Supreme Court in 1959, the Department of Justice in its brief said, "the OASI [Old-Age and Survivors Insurance] program is in no sense a federally-administered insurance program under which each worker pays premiums over the years and acquires at retirement an indefeasible right to receive a fixed monthly benefit. The contributions exacted, are a tax."

Many people also have the mistaken impression that Social Security benefits are paid out of accumulated reserves, similar to private insurance programs, when in truth the program is financed almost entirely on a pay-as-you-go basis, with the benefits paid out of current income. Pay-as-you-go means that the government raises, through current taxes, just enough money to pay the cost of the benefits currently due. No one prepays his own benefits. Today's taxpayers pay for today's beneficiaries.

The acceptance of the King Bill would actually mean that our children and grandchildren will be asked to pay ever increasing Social Security taxes to finance the medical-care needs of the previous generations. With growing families, young people have enough difficulty trying to make ends meet without assuming the additional obligation of paying higher taxes to pay for the medical-care needs of all over sixty-five, many of whom are in better financial shape than those paying the tax.

Now this is the choice we're faced with: on the one hand, we can help those who need help while preserving the right of the self-reliant to finance their own care. Or we can legislate a compulsory national health scheme for the aged, regardless of whether they need it or not.

To put this choice in even sharper focus, Americans are being asked to choose between a system of medicine practiced in freedom and a system of socialized medicine for the elderly which will be expanded into socialized medicine for every man, woman, and child in the United States.

Your letter will help determine the outcome of this struggle. Remember what Ronald Reagan said:

[Reagan's voice]

Write those letters now. Call your friends, and tell them to write them. If you don't, this program I promise you will pass just as surely as the sun will come up tomorrow. And behind it will come other federal programs that will invade every area of freedom as we have known it in this country, until, one day, as Norman Thomas said, we will awake to find that we have socialism. And if you don't do this, and if I don't do it, one of these days, you and I are going to spend our sunset years telling our children, and our children's children, what it once was like in America when men were free.

Notes

Chapter 1

1. Eric Adler, "I Do, I Do: Some Days It's Just One Wedding After Another for Courthouse Preacher," *Kansas City Star*, 30 September 1998, p. F2.

2. Marilyn Moon, "Are Social Security Benefits Too High or Too Low?" in *Social Security in the 21st Century*, ed. Eric R. Kingson and James H. Schulz, (New York: Oxford University Press, 1977), p. 72.

3. Report of the 1994–1996 Advisory Council on Social Security, p. 89; see Robert M. Ball and Thomas N. Bethell, "Bridging the Centuries: The Case for Traditional Social Security," in *Social Security in the 21st Century*, ed. Kingson and Schulz, p. 277; see also Robert Eisner, *Social Security: More, Not Less* (New York: Century Foundation Press, 1998), p. 9.

4. *1998 Annual Report of the Board of Trustees of the Federal Old-Age and Survivors Insurance and Disability Trust Funds*, pp. 2 and 7.

5. See Thomas W. Jones, "Social Security: Invaluable, Irreplaceable, and Fixable," *The Participant* (February 1996), p. 4.

6. *1991 Annual Report of the Board of Trustees of the Federal Old-Age and Survivors Insurance and Disability Insurance Trust Funds*, p. 3.

7. Ibid., p. 38.

8. Ibid.

9. *1998 Annual Report of the Board of Trustees of the Federal Old-Age and Survivors Insurance and Disability Insurance Trust Funds*, p. 24.

10. Ibid., p. 92.

11. *1991 Annual Report*, p. 38.

12. Susan Dentzer, discussion in *Framing the Social Security Debate: Values, Politics, and Economics*, ed. R. Douglas Arnold,

Michael J. Graetz, and Alice H. Munnell (Washington: National Academy of Social Insurance, 1998), p. 420.

13. Ibid., p. 421.

14. *1998 Report*, p. 11.

15. Ibid., p. 57.

16. Ibid., p. 193.

17. Barry Bosworth, "What Economic Role for the Trust Funds?" in *Social Security in the 21st Century*, ed. Kingson and Schulz, p. 175.

18. Ball and Bethell, "Bridging the Centuries," p. 277.

19. Jones, "Social Security: Invaluable, Irreplaceable, and Fixable," p. 4.

20. Moon, "Are Social Security Benefits Too High or Too Low?" pp. 65–72.

Chapter 2

1. See Karl Mannheim, preface to *Diagnosis of Our Time* (New York: Oxford University Press, 1944), p. vii.

2. See Clarke Chambers, *Seedtime of Reform* (Minneapolis: University of Minnesota Press, 1963), pp. 3–11.

3. I. M. Rubinow, *Social Insurance* (New York: Henry Holt, 1913), p. 6.

4. Chambers, *Seedtime of Reform*, p. 89.

5. See Odin W. Anderson, "Compulsory Medical Care Insurance, 1910–1950,"*Annals of the American Academy of Political and Social Science* 273 (January 1951): 106–113.

6. Chambers, *Seedtime of Reform*, p. 158.

7. John D. Hicks, *Republican Ascendancy* (New York: Harper and Row, 1960), p. 73.

8. Irving Bernstein, *The Lean Years: A History of the American Worker, 1920–1933* (Boston: Houghton Mifflin, 1960), p. 237.

9. Paul Douglas, *Social Security in the United States* (New York: McGraw-Hill, 1939), pp. 5–7.

10. For an extensive discussion of the danger signals apparent in the 1920s, see Chambers, *Seedtime of Reform*, pp. 93–180.

11. Bernstein, *Lean Years*, p. 475.

12. Abraham Epstein, *Insecurity: A Challenge to America*, rev. ed. (New York: Harrison Smith and Robert Haas, 1936), pp. 22–23.

13. I. M. Rubinow, *The Quest for Security* (New York: H. Holt, 1934), pp. 520–521.

14. Martha Derthick, *Agency Under Stress* (Washington: Brookings Institution, 1990), p. 212, n. 4.

Chapter 3

1. Arthur M. Schlesinger, Jr., *The Age of Roosevelt: The Coming of the New Deal* (Boston: Houghton Mifflin, 1959), p. 298.

2. Bernstein, *Lean Years*, p. 475.

3. Ralph E. and Muriel W. Pumphrey, eds., *The Heritage of American Social Work* (New York: Columbia University Press, 1961), p. 439n.

4. See Douglas, *Social Security in the United States*, Chapter 4, for an excellent legislative history of the Social Security Act.

5. Committee on Economic Security, *Social Security in America: The Background of the Social Security Act as Summarized from Staff Reports to the Committee on Economic Security* (Washington: Government Printing Office, 1937), pp. 212–213.

6. Max J. Skidmore, *Medicare and the American Rhetoric of Reconciliation* (Tuscaloosa: University of Alabama Press, 1970), p. 60; voting figures from *Congressional Record*, 74th Congress, 1st session, pp. 9648–9650 and 6069–6070.

7. The next few paragraphs rely heavily on my 1970 *Medicare*, cited in the previous note, pp. 52–64.

8. For complete party platforms for 1936 and the next two decades, see Kirk Porter and Donald Johnson, *National Party Platforms, 1840–1956* (Urbana: University of Illinois Press, 1956).

9. "New Deal Blocking Jobs, Says Landon," *New York Times*, 8 May 1936.

10. "Scores Republicans on Security Attacks," *New York Times*, 1 November 1936.

11. Robert and Helen Lynd, *Middletown in Transition* (New York: Harcourt, Brace, and World, 1937), p. 361.

12. *Washington Herald*, 28 May 1936.

13. *New York Herald Tribune*, 29 September 1936.

14. Ibid., 2 November 1936.

15. *New York Times,* "Issues, Principles To Guide Business," 30 August 1936.

16. Laurence E. Davies, "Burden On Earner Held Lower Now," *New York Times,* 30 December 1939.

17. *Collier's,* 28 November 1936, p. 66.

18. "Aldrich Assails Profits Tax Bill," *New York Times,* 8 May 1936.

19. "Asks Security Act to Be Voided By Court, Stockholder in Boston Suit Says It and State Jobless Law 'Seize Property,'" *New York Times,* 1 November 1936, p. 28.

20. Douglas, *Social Security in the United States,* p. 1.

21. Hadley Cantril, ed., *Public Opinion, 1935–1946* (Princeton: Princeton University Press, 1951), p. 541.

Chapter 4

1. Morris Fishbein, M.D., *A History of the American Medical Association* (Philadelphia: W. B. Saunders, 1947), pp. 318–321.

2. "The American Medical Association: Power, Purpose and Politics in Organized Medicine," *Yale Law Journal,* 63 (May 1954): 1008; my discussion of the AMA's anti-Medicare propaganda activities through 1953 relies heavily on this invaluable study. For excellent summaries of proposed federal health-insurance legislation into the 1950s, see esp. pp. 1007–1018; see also Agnes W. Brewster, *Health Insurance and Related Proposals for Financing Personal Health Services* (Washington: U.S. Department of Health, Education, and Welfare: Social Security Administration, 1958).

3. "Power, Purpose and Politics," p. 1009; esp. footnote 602.

4. Ibid.

5. Ibid.

6. Ibid., pp. 1011–1014.

7. Ibid., p. 1016.

8. Ibid., p. 1017; see footnote 676.

9. *Journal of the American Medical Association* 181 (21 July 1962): 265.

10. *PR Reporter,* 28 May 1962, pp. 1–2; this publication described itself as "a working newsletter for public relations professionals."

11. Ibid.

12. Ibid.

13. See *We Support Health Benefits for the Aged through Social Security* (New York: National Association of Social Workers, 1961), for a list of organizations and prominent persons supporting the Anderson-King Bill.

14. U.S. Congress, *Health Services for the Aged Under the Social Security Insurance System*, Hearings before the Ways and Means Committee (Washington: U.S. Government Printing Office, 1961), pp. 701–702 (cited hereafter as "Hearings").

15. Blue Shield plans are generally the creations of medical societies; the National Blue Shield Plan was separate from the Blue Cross Association and was closely allied with the AMA.

16. See Max J. Skidmore, "Operation Coffeecup: A Hidden Episode in American Political History," *Journal of American Culture* 12 (Fall 1989): 89–96.

17. Thanks to my doctoral student, Phil Black, whose Internet skills and connections in the medical community enabled him to locate it, I now have a tape of the recording.

Chapter 5

1. Richard C. Leone, "Stick with Public Pensions," *Foreign Affairs* 76 (July/August 1997): 41.

2. Peter G. Peterson, "Will America Grow Up Before it Grows OLD?" *Atlantic Monthly* 277 (May 1996): 57.

3. Robert Eisner, "What Social Security Crisis?" *Wall Street Journal*, 30 August 1996.

4. Peter Passell, "Can Retirees' Safety Net Be Saved?" *New York Times*, 18 February 1996, sec. 3, p. 1.

5. Peterson, "Will America Grow Up?" pp. 55–86, esp. pp. 75–82.

6. James K. Glassman, "The Only Workable Solution for Social Security Is to Make It Private," *Kansas City Star*, 10 September 1995, sec. J, p. 5.

7. Mark Thornton, "Abolish Social Security," *USA Today*, 4 January 1996, sec. A, p. 8.

8. Eisner, "What Social Security Crisis?"; see also his *Social Security: More, Not Less.*

9. Eisner, *Social Security: More, Not Less,* Chapters 4 and 5.

10. Passell, "Can Retirees' Safety Net Be Saved?" pp. 1, 4.

Chapter 6

1. Skidmore, *Medicare,* p. 131.

2. Kurt Ritter, "Ronald Reagan and 'The Speech': The Rhetoric of Public Relations Politics," *Western Speech,* 32: no. 1 (Winter 1968); reprinted in Max J. Skidmore, *Word Politics: Essays on Language and Politics,* Palo Alto: James A. Freel and Associates, 1972, pp. 110–118.

3. The text of the Phoenix speech, "Encroaching Control," is available at the Reagan Collection of the Hoover Institution at Stanford University. It is virtually the same as the Orange County speech, "Encroaching Control: Keep Government Poor and Remain Free," in *Vital Speeches of the Day* 37 (1 September 1961): 678.

4. Ronald Reagan, "Free Enterprise," *Vital Speeches* 39 (15 January 1973): 200–201.

5. Ronnie Dugger, *On Reagan: The Man and His Presidency* (New York: McGraw-Hill, 1983), pp. 49–50.

6. Ibid., p. 43.

7. Laurence I. Barrett, *Gambling with History: Ronald Reagan in the White House* (Garden City, N.Y.: Doubleday, 1983), p. 156.

8. David A. Stockman, *The Triumph of Politics* (New York: Avon Books, 1987), p. 175.

9. Barrett, *Gambling with History,* p. 63.

10. Kevin Phillips, *The Politics of Rich and Poor* (New York: Random House, 1990), p. 80.

11. *Annual Report,* Washington: Americans for Generational Equity, 1990, p. 2.

12. Jill Quadagno, "Generational Equity and the Politics of the Welfare State," *Politics and Society* 17, no. 3 (1989): 2.

13. Peter Peterson and Neil Howe, *On Borrowed Time: How the Growth of Entitlements Threatens America's Future* (San Francisco: Institute for Contemporary Studies, 1988), p. 43.

14. Theodore R. Marmor, Fay Lomax Cook, and Stephen Scher, "Social Security Politics and the Conflict Between Generations: Are We Asking the Right Questions?" in *Social Security in the 21st Century,* ed. Kingson and Schulz, p. 204.

15. Trudy Lieberman, "Social Insecurity: The Campaign to Take the System Private," *The Nation* 264 (27 January 1997): 11–18.

16. Ibid., p. 14.

17. Ibid., p. 13.

18. Lawrence R. Jacobs and Robert Y. Shapiro, "Myth and Misunderstandings about Public Opinion and Social Security," in *Framing the Social Security Debate*, ed. R. Douglas Arnold, Michael J. Graetz, and Alice Munnell (Washington: National Academy of Social Insurance, 1998), pp. 355–388.

19. Ibid., p. 364.

20. Ibid., p. 357.

21. See Lieberman, "Social Insecurity," p. 14.

22. Ibid., p. 13.

23. Ibid., pp. 15–18.

24. Richard C. Leone, "Stick with Public Pensions," *Foreign Affairs* 76, no. 4 (July/August 1997): 46.

25. Lieberman, "Social Insecurity," p. 16.

26. Stephen Winn, "Despite the 'Surplus,' Our National Debt Still Grows," *Kansas City Star*, 4 October 1998, sec. K, p. 1.

27. Lieberman, "Social Insecurity," p. 16.

28. Fred Brock, "Save Social Security? From What?" *New York Times*, 1 November 1998, p. 12.

29. "The Impeachment Breather," *New York Times*, 1 November 1998, p. 14.

30. Lieberman, "Social Insecurity," pp. 16 and 18.

31. Jack Anderson, "Why Should I Pay for People Who Don't Need It?," *Parade*, 21 February 1993.

32. Rich Thomas, "Why Cutting Entitlements Makes Sense," *Newsweek*, 31 May 1993.

33. Virginia P. Reno and Robert B. Friedland, "Strong Support but Low Confidence," in *Social Security in the 21st Century*, ed. Kingson and Schulz, p. 188.

34. See my "Public Integrity: Perspectives from Home and Abroad," *Public Integrity Annual* (Council of State Governments/ American Society for Public Administration) 1 (April 1996): 107–114.

Chapter 7

1. John Zvesper, "The Liberal Rhetoric of Franklin Roosevelt," in *Rhetoric and American Statesmanship*, ed. Glen Thurow and Jeffry

Wallin (Durham, NC: Carolina Academic Press and Claremont Institute for the Study of Statesmanship and Political Philosophy, 1984), p. 87.

2. David Potter, *People of Plenty: Economic Abundance and the American Character* (Chicago: University of Chicago Press, 1954), p. 123; quoted in Skidmore, *Medicare*, p. 4. The next few paragraphs draw extensively on this latter work.

3. William E. Leuchtenburg, *Franklin D. Roosevelt and the New Deal, 1932–1940* (New York: Harper and Row, 1963), p. 165.

4. See Jill Quadagno, *The Transformation of Old Age Security: Class and Politics in the American Welfare State* (Chicago: University of Chicago Press, 1988), p. 121.

5. Basil Rauch, ed., *Franklin D. Roosevelt: Selected Speeches, Messages, Press Conferences, and Letters* (New York: Rinehart and Co., 1957), pp. 161–162.

6. Ibid., pp. 144–145.

7. Robert H. Bremner, "The New Deal and Social Welfare," in *Fifty Years Later: The New Deal Evaluated*, ed. Harvard Sitkoff (Philadelphia: Temple University Press, 1985), p. 69.

8. Ibid., p. 77.

9. Ibid.

10. Frank Freidel, *The New Deal in Historical Perspective* (Washington: Service Center for Teachers of History of the American Historical Association, 1959), p. 3.

11. See the discussion in Freidel, *The New Deal*, pp. 13–14.

12. Bremner, "The New Deal and Social Welfare," pp. 88–89.

13. See William E. Leuchtenburg, "The Achievement of the New Deal," in *Fifty Years Later*, ed. Sitkoff, p. 220.

14. Fred L. Israel, ed., *The State of the Union Messages of the Presidents*, vol. 3 (New York: Chelsea House Publishers, 1967), p. 2840.

15. Rauch, ed., *FDR: Selected Speeches*, p. 351.

16. Ibid., pp. 363–364.

17. *Vital Speeches* 14 (1 July 1948): 531.

18. Ibid., p. 552.

19. *Vital Speeches* 15 (15 January 1949): 196.

20. *Vital Speeches* 15 (15 September 1949): 707.

21. *Vital Speeches* 18 (15 April 1952): 387.

22. "The Middle Road," an address delivered in Boise, Idaho, on 20 August 1952; *Vital Speeches* 18 (1 September 1952): 677.

23. See *Vital Speeches* 19 (1 February 1953): 252–254.

24. *Vital Speeches* 19 (15 February 1953): 264.

25. *Vital Speeches* 20 (1 February 1954): 230.

26. Ibid., p. 231.

27. *Vital Speeches* 21 (15 January 1955): 966.

28. *Vital Speeches* 22 (1 February 1956): 231.

29. "What Is the Job to Be Done?" Address to a Lexington, Kentucky, rally on 1 October 1956; *Vital Speeches* 23 (15 October 1956): 3.

30. *Vital Speeches* 27 (1 February 1961): 226–227.

31. Ibid., p. 237.

32. See Skidmore, *Medicare,* pp. 96–167.

33. *Vital Speeches* 28 (1 February 1962): 231.

34. *Vital Speeches* 28 (15 June 1962): 515–516.

35. See Skidmore, *Medicare,* pp. 129–131; as noted earlier, the AMA took no position in its official testimony before Congress regarding passage of the Social Security Act.

36. *Vital Speeches* 30 (15 January 1964): 194–195.

37. *Vital Speeches* 30 (15 September 1964): 709–710.

38. "The Wants of the People," Labor Day address in Detroit on 7 September 1964; *Vital Speeches* 30 (1 October 1964): 742.

39. "The Great Society"; *Vital Speeches* 31 (15 January 1965): 196.

40. *Vital Speeches* 33 (1 February 1967): 226–228.

41. "Speech to AFL-CIO Convention, Bal Harbour, Florida, 12 December 1967"; *Vital Speeches* 34 (1 January 1968): 162–163.

42. *Vital Speeches* 34 (1 February 1968): 228.

43. *Vital Speeches* 35 (1 February 1969): 228.

44. *Vital Speeches* 36 (1 January 1970): 162.

45. *Vital Speeches* 37 (1 February 1971): 227.

46. *Vital Speeches* 38 (15 September 1972): 707.

47. Frank Kessler, *The Dilemmas of Presidential Leadership: Of Caretakers and Kings* (Englewood Cliffs, NJ: Prentice-Hall, 1982), pp. 313–314.

48. *Vital Speeches* 39 (15 March 1973): 325–326.

49. *Vital Speeches* 61 (1 February 1975): 227.

50. See Johnson's comment in his State of the Union message on 17 January 1968; *Vital Speeches* 34 (1 February 1968): 229.

51. *Vital Speeches* 42 (1 February 1976): 228.

52. Ibid.

53. *Vital Speeches* 42 (15 September 1976): 708.

54. *Vital Speeches* 43 (1 February 1977): 226–230.

55. *Vital Speeches* 66 (15 September 1980): 706–710.

56. *Vital Speeches* 67 (15 March 1981): 323.

Chapter 8

1. See Beth C. Fuchs and Mark Merlis, *CRS Report for Congress: Health Care Reform: President Clinton's Health Security Act* (Washington: Congressional Research Service, Library of Congress, 22 November 1993); this source gives complete details of the proposed plan.

2. Haynes Johnson and David S. Broder, *The System: The American Way of Politics at the Breaking Point* (New York: Little, Brown, 1996).

3. Ibid., p. 584.

4. Ibid., p. 588.

5. Ibid., p. 602.

6. David Gergen, "And Now, the Fifth Estate?" *U.S. News and World Report* (28 April 1966), p. 84.

7. Ibid.

8. Johnson and Broder, *The System*, p. 603.

Chapter 9

1. Milton Friedman, "Social Security Chimeras," *New York Times*, 11 January 1999.

Suggestions for Further Reading

Henry J. Aaron, ed. *The Problem that Won't Go Away: Reforming U.S. Health Care Financing.* Washington: Brookings Institution, 1996. A collection of articles on health care financing and Medicare.

Henry Aaron, Barry P. Bosworth, and Gary Burtless. *Can America Afford to Grow Old?: Paying for Social Security.* Washington: Brookings Institution, 1989. A readable examination of the economic issues pertaining to Social Security.

R. Douglas Arnold, Michael J. Graetz, and Alicia H. Munnell, eds. *Framing the Social Security Debate: Values, Politics, and Economics.* Washington: National Academy of Social Insurance, 1998. An extensive collection of some of the most insightful studies by specialists on Social Security

Robert M. Ball, *Social Security: Today and Tomorrow.* New York: Columbia University Press, 1978. Presentation of the basic issues regarding Social Security by one of the foremost experts, a former—and long-time—commissioner of Social Security.

Robert M. Ball with Thomas N. Bethell. *Straight Talk about Social Security: An Analysis of the Issues in the Current Debate.* New York: The Century Foundation Press, 1998. Analysis of current issues by a highly respected former commissioner of Social Security.

Edward D. Berkowitz. *America's Welfare State: From Roosevelt to Reagan.* Baltimore: Johns Hopkins University Press, 1991.

Merton C. Bernstein and Joan Brodshaug Bernstein. *Social Security: The System that Works.* New York: Basic Books, 1988. A theoretical analysis of the system, including ancillary issues.

Robert Eisner. *Social Security: More, Not Less.* New York: Century Foundation Press, 1998—brief but insightful suggestions for Social Security by one of the few analysts who has recognized the propaganda for what it is.

Into the Twenty-First Century: The Development of Social Security. Geneva: International Labour Office, 1984. A valuable discussion of basic principles applicable to various national systems.

Eric R. Kingson and Edward D. Berkowitz. *Social Security and Medicare: A Policy Primer.* Westport, Conn.: Auburn House, 1993. A thoughtful attempt at presenting a balanced view of the issues involved in Social Security.

Eric R. Kingson and James H. Schulz. *Social Security in the 21st Century.* New York: Oxford University Press, 1997. An excellent collection of readings by specialists in social insurance.

Peter A. Köhler, F. Zacher, and Martin Partington. *The Evolution of Social Insurance, 1881–1991.* London: Frances Pinter Publishers, 1982. A comparative analysis of European systems.

Paul Light. *Artful Work: The Politics of Social Security Reform.* New York: Random House, 1985. Insightful discussion of the political issues involved.

Robert J. Myers. *Social Security,* 4th ed. Philadelphia: Wharton School/University of Pennsylvania Press, 1993. An encyclopedic source of information, written by a former long-time chief actuary for the Social Security Administration.

John Myles. *Old Age in the Welfare State: The Political Economy of Public Pensions.* Lawrence: University Press of Kansas, 1989. Theoretical perspectives on financing and related issues.

Ann Shola Orloff. *The Politics of Pensions: A Comparative Analysis of Britain, Canada, and the United States, 1880–1940.* Madison: University of Wisconsin Press 1993.

Henry J. Pratt. *Gray Agendas: Interest Groups and Public Pensions in Canada, Britain, and the United States.* Ann Arbor: University of Michigan Press, 1993. Theory and analysis by a specialist in matters pertaining to the aged.

Max J. Skidmore. *Medicare and the American Rhetoric of Reconciliation.* Tuscaloosa: University of Alabama Press, 1970. An examination of the controversies surrounding the adoption of Social Security and Medicare.

C. Eugene Steuerle and Jon M. Bakija. *Retooling Social Security for the 21st Century: Right and Wrong Approaches to Reform.* Washington: The Urban Institute Press, 1994. An extensive collection of essays and articles on Social Security, rather traditional in its approach.

Malcolm G. Taylor. *Insuring National Health Care: The Canadian Experience.* Chapel Hill: University of North Carolina Press, 1990.

John B. Williamson and Fred C. Pampel. *Old-Age Security in Comparative Perspective.* New York: Oxford University Press, 1993. A cross-national analysis of selected systems in Europe, Asia, South America, Africa, and the United States.

Index